WALCH PUBLISHING

Critical Thinking
Readings in Nonfiction

Middle School

Second Edition

Donald L. Barnes,
Thomas S. Schroeder,
and Arlene Burgdorf

1   2   3   4   5   6   7   8   9   10

ISBN 978-0-8251-6274-9

Copyright © 1992, 2002
J. Weston Walch, Publisher
P.O. Box 658 • Portland, Maine 04104-0658
www.walch.com

Printed in the United States of America

Contents

To the Teacher

Ever since the days of Socrates and Aristotle, teachers have cherished the hope that they can somehow unravel the mysteries of rational thought and help students to cultivate their inherent powers of observation, deliberation, and reflection. The search for a basic understanding of cognitive functions, however, has been frustrating. Even today, in the twenty-first century, scientists hold widely varying views on how human thought processes are triggered and how the brain controls and facilitates the flow of information.

George Johnson, a science editor for the *New York Times,* has described current investigations into human memory and reasoning in his book *In the Palaces of Memory: How We Build the Worlds Inside Our Heads* (Knopf, 1991). It is evident from Johnson's comprehensive review as well as other research studies that the facts are not all in regarding how the mind stores and retrieves data.

Why Thinking Skills Are Important

Despite our limited knowledge of how humans process information, we can ill afford to neglect the teaching of thinking skills. There are at least four compelling reasons for us to take this task seriously:

1. Every child can benefit from this type of instruction. No child is devoid of critical-thinking competencies, and no child has developed these skills so fully that there isn't some area in his or her life in which hazy, inconsistent thinking still dominates.

2. Self-interest dictates much of human behavior. We have a penchant for using our cognitive and affective processes to justify selfish motives and to undermine opposing interpretations of events. Critical thinking can help us learn to see merit in competing points of view and consider more fully the welfare of others.

3. People in all age groups have a natural disinclination to recognize the degree to which they have failed to develop critical-thinking competencies. They will readily admit that they cannot play the piano or repair a TV, for these limitations are self-evident. However, these same people tend to view critical thinking, like talking or walking, as a competency we all use at about the same level.

4. Modern personal, community, and world problems are so complex that they demand our very best thinking. Today we face a bewildering variety of political, social, and economic challenges. We must have an intellectually alert citizenry to address these perplexing, often overwhelming, dilemmas.

Selecting Materials and Strategies

There are, of course, a large number of critical-thinking tests from which to choose. The *Watson-Glaser* and the *Cornell Critical Thinking Test* are probably the best known. The former emphasizes inference, assumptions, deduction, interpretation, and evaluation of arguments; the latter focuses on hypotheses, deduction, reliability of authorities, assumptions, and relevance. There is also a wide variety of thinking-skills programs. These include *Structure of the Intellect* (Mary Meeker), *Instrumental Enrichment* (Rueven Feuerstein), *Philosophy for Children* (Matthew Lipman), *Chicago Mastery Learning* (Beau Fly Jones), and *Strategic Reasoning* (John Glade). These programs serve somewhat different purposes and widely diverse age groups; however, they all tend to emphasize the direct teaching of cognitive skills.

This book focuses on the direct teaching of skills in seven areas:

1. Judging the Relevance of Information for Specific Purposes

2. Distinguishing Among Facts, Assumptions, and Values

3. Understanding How Conditions or Events in a Story or Report Relate to Each Other

4. Recognizing Cause-Effect Relationships

5. Understanding the Rules of Rational Thinking

6. Identifying Persuasive Techniques

7. Recognizing the Writer's Assumptions

Open-ended, interactive Follow-up Activities have been added for each of these seven areas.

These activities appear in this Teacher's Guide at the end of the answer key for each section.

No program of critical-thinking and reasoning competencies can address more than a fraction of the cognitive skills needed for academic success and daily problem solving. The preceding list, however, represents a good mix of basic competencies that are relevant to a wide variety of common problematic situations. We cannot approach even the simplest task without first judging the relevance of information. We cannot read a newspaper intelligently without separating facts from values and understanding how the events in the news stories relate to each other. We can hardly get to first base in any area of science without first understanding cause-effect relationships and recognizing how fallacies in thinking can rob us of our objectivity. We cannot participate intelligently in political elections or respond to advertising without understanding something about persuasive techniques and writers' assumptions.

This book cannot make reflective thinkers out of students who are just beginning to test the boundaries of rational thought, but the stories and problematic situations it offers can serve as springboards to interesting discussions and help students recognize and cultivate their inherent powers of intellectual inquiry.

> The authors would like to thank Dana Slayback and Jill Rager for their work on question formats in this book.

To the Student

You may have heard that the story of *Robinson Crusoe* by Daniel Defoe is based on the real-life adventures of a Scottish sailor named Alexander Selkirk. While Selkirk was serving as first mate on the British ship *Cinque Ports* in the South Pacific, he had a violent argument with the captain. Selkirk was so distressed that he asked to leave the ship at one of the uninhabited Juan Fernandez islands off the coast of Chile. He remained alone on the island for 52 months, from 1704 to 1709. He was rescued by another English vessel under the command of Captain Woods Rogers.

During his 52 months on the island, Selkirk had to use his wits to survive. Although he took some clothes, a hatchet, a pistol, gunpowder, and bullets when he left the ship, these supplies soon gave out. He had to plan and build out of scraps of wood and branches a hut that would withstand the sea breezes. He had to chase down and capture wild goats. He ate goat meat and made clothes from the skins of the goats. He even learned to tame several of the animals so that he could enjoy their companionship. If Selkirk had not developed basic survival skills, he would not have lived to tell his story.

You, too, need to develop basic "survival skills" if you hope to succeed in today's world. We now live in the Age of Information, and we must learn to recognize and sort ideas quickly if we are going to keep up with changing job markets and world events. The seven basic skill areas practiced in this book can help you deal successfully with a wide variety of academic challenges and everyday problematic situations. As you sharpen your skills in judging the relevance of information and distinguishing between facts and values, and as you learn to relate events in stories and reports, you will better understand the things you read. As you strengthen your understanding of cause-effect relationships and the rules of rational thinking, you will better comprehend the worlds of science. As you learn to identify persuasive techniques and writers' assumptions, you will be able to grasp the significant ideas offered in political debates and advertising campaigns.

There is no shortcut to good, clear, logical thinking. If there were a simple method of producing brilliant people, we would have been turning out superb scientists, talented writers, and clever political leaders like pancakes over the years. The road to better thinking may be difficult at times, but the end results are well worth the effort.

I.

Getting to the Heart of the Matter:

Judging the Relevance of Information for Specific Purposes

Introduction

When you judge the *relevance* of information, you try to decide whether specific facts or knowledge will be helpful in solving a problem. Let's assume, for example, that the heat has been turned off in your neighbor's home, and you are trying to get into the house to rescue your neighbor's parakeet. A little girl tells you that she knows where the key to the back door is kept. This is *relevant* information because it helps you solve the problem. If, on the other hand, the little girl tells you that the parakeet's name is Fluff, this is *not* relevant information because it does not help you rescue the bird.

If your brother is trying to earn money, and the man next door tells you that the car wash is employing young people, this is *relevant* information. Even if your brother applies for the job and doesn't get it, the information is still *relevant* because it might have helped him with his problem—earning money. *Relevant* information doesn't automatically solve the problem, but it is clearly related to finding a solution.

Read each of the situations listed below and decide whether the information provided is *relevant* to the solution of the problem. Write YES in the blank if it is *relevant* or NO if it is *not relevant*.

_____ 1. Chuck Thompson is trying to build a model of a castle on a large table in his basement. Jerry, his best friend, offers to show Chuck pictures of knights that he has collected. Is the pictorial information Jerry offers *relevant?*

_____ 2. Andy Chang is making posters for a Fourth of July celebration. Kim Mandarin offers to show Andy how to write the posters in Chinese. Is the information Kim offers *relevant* information?

_____ 3. Ralph Rigley is trying to patch his football before his friends come to practice. They can't use it because it is too soft. Jimmy Black offers to bring his football to the practice so the boys won't be disappointed. Is Jimmy's offer *relevant* to the solution of the problem?

_____   4. Randy Jacobs broke his finger and can't play basketball. His little cousin next door offers to show Randy how he can revive a person who has stopped breathing. Is the information offered by his cousin *relevant*?

_____   5. You are trying to buy a small TV set for your sister for her birthday, and you don't have much money. Your mother gives you an advertisement from an electronic-equipment store that is offering all kinds of items at reduced cost. Is the information your mother offers *relevant*?

_____   6. Your aunt is trying to find a safe place to teach swimming and aquatic skills. Her husband mentions that Lake Omega is listed as one of the most beautiful bodies of water in the region. Is the information her husband offers *relevant*?

_____   7. Art Thompson is looking for something to do after school on Wednesdays. Tom Radcliffe tells him that the navy is looking for new recruits. Is the information Tom offers *relevant*?

In the following exercises, you will be asked a series of questions related to a short article. You must determine which information in the article is relevant to each question, and which information is not relevant.

The Statue of Liberty

In 1865, a writer, Edouard de Laboulaye, and a sculptor, Frederic Bartholdi, met at a banquet near Versailles (ver sī′), France. They discussed the possibility of having the French make a statue to present to the American people on the 100th birthday of American independence, if the United States would provide the statue's pedestal.

Nothing was settled then, but in 1871, Bartholdi made a trip to the United States. He presented letters of introduction to many important people, including President Grant, leading industrialists, literary figures, and religious leaders in his effort to persuade them to support his idea for a united French-American effort in this project. He noticed that Bedloe's Island, a 12-acre tract southwest of the tip of Manhattan, would be an excellent place for the proposed statue. Unfortunately, Bartholdi received word from Washington that the French would have to take the first step in beginning the structure.

Although Bartholdi's plans were delayed by this decision, his enthusiasm was not dampened. Bartholdi and de Laboulaye worked in France for the next five years gaining support for their idea and planning the work. The Statue of Liberty was to be 152 feet high and weigh 225 tons. Her robes were to be fashioned from flowing sheets of copper.

The two men raised $400,000 in France. On May 6, 1876, Bartholdi left Paris with a French delegation to attend the Philadelphia Centennial Exhibition. The Statue of Liberty's torch arm was shown at the centennial celebration. Bartholdi and his statue gained much attention in American newspapers and magazines. Bartholdi returned to France and continued work on the statue. Many fund-raisers in France kept the project moving.

The United States' progress for the statue was not as successful, however. In this country, the publisher Joseph Pulitzer headed a drive to fund the pedestal. Pulitzer used editorials in his newspaper to persuade Americans, especially rich ones, to financially support the building of a pedestal. He emphasized that refusing to support the project would be refusing a gift of sentiment and generosity from a friendly nation. Pulitzer also announced that any donor's name, rich or poor, would be printed on the pedestal as a public recognition. He eventually collected $270,000.

In 1884, the statue's interior and exterior were taken apart piece by piece and packed into 200 mammoth crates. In May 1885, the Statue of Liberty sailed to America aboard the ship *Isere*.

When President Cleveland presided over the inauguration of the statue on October 28, 1886, the famous verse welcoming immigrants to our country was not yet in place. It was finally added in 1905.

In 1976, the Statue of Liberty was given a complete overhaul for the 200th anniversary of America's independence. Fittingly, French workers helped in making the Statue of Liberty almost new once again.

Read each question. Then circle the letter of the best answer to each question.

1. On his first trip to the United States, Bartholdi presented his idea to many influential people. Suppose you had to choose the people with whom Bartholdi should speak. What information would be LEAST important in your decision?

   a. Information concerning the accomplishments of the person

   b. Information concerning the popularity of this person within the country

   c. Information concerning the authority this person has in making decisions that could affect the project

   d. Information concerning the number of American people this person can influence

2. You must decide what part of the statue should be displayed at the Philadelphia Centennial Exhibition. This exhibition will be an opportunity for the statue to gain publicity, and you want to select a part that will remain in the minds of those who see it. What information would be MOST important to consider?

   a. Information concerning the cost of shipping the part to the exhibition

   b. Information concerning the eye appeal of the part you will send

   c. Information concerning the materials needed to build the part

3. Joseph Pulitzer's initial campaign to raise funds for the Statue of Liberty's pedestal was not successful, but as his newspaper grew, he decided to try again. He published more articles informing people of the pedestal's progress and the need for funding. Which of the following information would have been LEAST relevant to Pulitzer's decision to try again?

   a. Because of an ultimatum stating that the pedestal would be built in another city if funds were not raised, people's interest in the project was renewed.

   b. Pulitzer's newspaper had gained many more readers since its coverage of the presidential election.

   c. The newspaper was two pages longer than it had been during the first fund-raising attempt.

4. You are a reader of Joseph Pulitzer's newspaper. When Pulitzer attempted to raise money for the pedestal the first time, you gave money. You regretted it when politicians began talking about moving the statue to another city. What information would NOT be helpful in convincing you to donate the second time?

   a. Information published about the people who had donated money both times

   b. Information published about the continuing construction of the pedestal because of new funds being brought in by Pulitzer's campaign

   c. Information published about the increased cost of building the pedestal

   d. Information suggesting that the project might not be supported by the French people

5. Bartholdi decided that Bedloe's Island would be an excellent site for the statue he wanted to build. What information do you think would have been MOST relevant to Bartholdi's decision?

   a. If placed on Bedloe's Island, the spectacular statue would serve as the first glimpse of America for many immigrants and visitors.

   b. The island would be hard to get to from New York City.

   c. The large population of New York City would easily be able to fund a pedestal for the statue.

6. You are a citizen of France. You must decide whether to support the idea of building the statue. Which of the following facts would NOT be helpful in persuading you to support the idea?

   a. The fact that the French have a keen appreciation for artistic work

   b. The fact that the Americans are not taking steps to prepare a pedestal for the work

   c. The fact that Bartholdi is a well-known, experienced sculptor

7. You are a member of a committee in France that must decide whether to support the Statue of Liberty project. Bartholdi appears before your committee to answer questions about the project. Which of the following questions is MOST relevant to the situation?

   a. What materials will be needed to build this statue?

   b. Will the Americans present us with a statue in return?

   c. How many French people live in America?

8. If you wanted to learn about building a statue, what kind of experience would be LEAST beneficial to you?

   a. Visiting the Statue of Liberty and walking all the way to the top

   b. Making miniature statues out of clay and other materials in an art class

   c. Reading a book about how Bartholdi convinced the French people to support his idea

9. The Statue of Liberty is enormous—it has an 8-foot index finger, a book 2 feet thick, and an arm 42 feet long! If you wanted to get a better understanding of the statue's size, but couldn't actually visit the statue, which experience would be MOST helpful?

   a. Studying pictures of the statue from many angles and viewpoints

   b. Going outside and measuring out the length of the finger, the thickness of the book, and the length of the arm

   c. Finding out the rest of the dimensions of the statue, such as the length of the nose, the waist size, and the total height of the statue

10. Joseph Pulitzer printed the names of all individuals who donated to the pedestal project regardless of the amount they gave. Many poor and common people gave small amounts to support the project, but many of the rich refused to donate. If you were preparing the list of donors for him, what information would be MOST relevant?

    a. Information about the amounts of money given by each person

    b. Information concerning where those who donated lived

    c. The correct spelling of each contributor's name

    d. The names of wealthy people who did not give

Developing the Parachute

Parachutes today are used in many ways. They are used in recreation, as emergency escape devices, and in the transportation of goods and people.

The true origin of parachuting can be traced to the work of 16th- and 17th-century scientists who studied gravity and velocity. These subjects are still helpful to contemporary developers of parachutes. Although the first parachute demonstration did not occur until 1783, Leonardo da Vinci discussed the principles involved as early as 1514. He sketched a cloth parachute that was designed to break a person's fall.

Even though da Vinci's principles were accurate, there was really no practical use for the parachute in his time. In the 18th and 19th centuries, however, hot-air balloons were developed. As balloons gained popularity, parachutes became more useful. Joseph and Jacques Montgolfier, while pursuing further developments with the hot-air balloon, used parachutes as emergency devices.

Louis-Sébastien Lenormand of France was the first person to demonstrate the simple canopy parachute. In 1783, he leaped from a high tower to a safe landing, using the device.

Four years later, an excited crowd gathered in Parc Monceau to watch André-Jacques Garnerin rise to 3,000 feet in the basket of a balloon. He then cut the cord and descended slowly to Earth with a parachute resembling an oversized umbrella. Garnerin visited various countries to exhibit his jump from ever-increasing heights. He made one jump from 8,000 feet in England.

As Garnerin made higher and higher jumps, he experienced swinging motions as the parachute descended. Garnerin would become violently ill after each swinging jump, but he could not explain or correct the problem. Finally, in 1804, Joseph Lalande, a scientist and astronomer, suggested cutting a hole in the top of the parachute to allow air to escape not only along the edges of the parachute (which was the cause of the swinging) but through the top as well.

The first parachutes were made of canvas. They were replaced by silk and then nylon, which is used today. A later development not considered in the earliest parachutes was the use of many little pieces of fabric to confine rips to small sections.

During World War I, hot-air balloons were used as lofty observation sites. The military provided its ballooning soldiers with parachute packs, but unfortunately many lives were lost due to the military's reluctance to issue parachutes to personnel in engine-powered aircraft. Military leaders were afraid that inexperienced pilots would jump before it was necessary, thereby wasting a repairable aircraft. Eventually, Germany realized that aircraft could be replaced more easily than seasoned pilots, and they began equipping their pilots with parachutes.

Although the first person to jump from a plane was Captain Albert Berry of the United States Army in 1912, it was not until 1918, just before the end of the war, that the United States began distributing parachutes regularly to its aircraft personnel. Colonel William "Billy" Mitchell recognized the potential of the new parachutes and proposed that they be used to conduct an "airborne assault" in which soldiers would be dropped to fight behind enemy lines.

Today developers have found that cargo of any weight or size can be transported from sky to Earth by parachute. Enormous parachutes helped the Apollo space capsule land in 1971. When a fighter plane is traveling at supersonic speeds, the pilot, seat, and parachute are ejected (thrown out) by a small rocket. The seat is discarded, and the parachute opens automatically.

Sport parachuting is presently enjoyed by over 30,000 Americans. Continued developments in the area of parachuting have made this sport quite safe. Modern parachutes with suspension lines are arranged into a pack. The rip cord may be released by hand, by a timing device, or by a line attached to a plane. Research reveals that most injuries occur when safe jumping practices are not followed. Sport parachuting has allowed many people to enjoy the same thrill of free flight that was experienced by pioneers of parachuting such as Louis-Sébastien Lenormand and André-Jacques Garnerin.

Read each question. Then circle the letter of the best answer to each question.

1. You want to make your own model parachute as accurate as possible. What information would be LEAST helpful in completing this task?

    a. Information about the types of fabrics used to make parachutes

    b. Information about the sizes and shapes of parachutes

    c. Information about the construction of a parachute

    d. Information about the amount of time a parachutist must wait before pulling the rip cord

2. If you wanted to learn the skill of sport parachuting, what experience would be MOST beneficial?

    a. Studying the models of the parachute Leonardo da Vinci designed, although no records show that it was ever used

    b. Observing how the parachute is packed at the factory in order for it to open correctly during your descent

    c. Studying and observing beginning jumping strategies used by experienced jumpers

3. Suppose that after observing one of André-Jacques Garnerin's swinging parachute jumps you decide to try to help him find a solution to the problem of the swinging. What information would NOT be useful in finding a solution?

    a. A study of the principles introduced by Leonardo da Vinci's parachute

    b. A study of the physical elements of air flow and resistance

    c. A study of the balloon Garnerin used to gain altitude in his jumps

4. Leonardo da Vinci designed his 16th-century parachute for escaping from a tall building that was burning, but the use of parachutes did not become common until the development of the hot-air balloon. What information would be LEAST relevant to an explanation of the parachute's delayed popularity?

    a. Information about the heights reached by the early hot-air balloons

    b. Information about the heights of buildings during Leonardo da Vinci's time

    c. Information about the safety of the early hot-air balloons

    d. Information about the materials used to make hot-air balloons

5. As mentioned in the story, parachutes were first made of canvas, then silk, and now nylon, which is a synthetic material. What information would be LEAST relevant in explaining these changes in fabric?

    a. The large quantities of silk needed to make a parachute were at first expensive to purchase.

    b. Nylon and silk are thin but strong fabrics that are easy to carry in a pack.

    c. The development of nylon took longest, because a great deal of research was needed to make nylon from coal.

    d. Canvas is a heavy, durable fabric that can withstand harsh winds and weather.

6. You are a military leader during World War I, and you must decide if it would be a good idea to purchase parachutes for not only the ballooning soldiers, but also the aircraft pilots. What information would be MOST useful in making a decision?

    a. Information concerning the success of Garnerin's jumps

    b. Information concerning the success of Germany's use of parachutes

    c. Information concerning the early development of parachutes

7. Suppose you are an astronaut aboard the Apollo space capsule. Months before the space capsule is to launch, you find out that parachutes will be assisting the capsule in landing. What information would be MOST relevant in helping you determine the safety of the landing strategy?

    a. Information concerning the types of "passengers" (people or objects) that have been dropped by parachute

    b. Information concerning the conditions in which parachutes have been used to send messages

    c. Information concerning whether the parachute can be used again

8. You want to do a science project demonstrating the principles of science used in parachuting. What information would be MOST useful to know?

    a. Information concerning the uses of parachutes in the military

    b. Information about the laws of gravity, air resistance, and velocity

    c. Information about the colors used for various kinds of parachutes

9. You have just developed a revolutionary new parachute. What step would be MOST appropriate to take before testing the parachute with a human parachutist?

    a. Make certain that the event is well publicized in order to gain recognition.

    b. Make certain that the parachute has been thoroughly tested with nonhuman "passengers."

    c. Make certain that the area where the event is to take place is well cleared and that an alternate landing site is available.

10. In the article, the author mentions three methods by which a rip cord can be released. As a beginning parachutist, you are told by your instructor to attach the line to the plane for your first jump rather than pull the rip cord by hand. Which explanation would be LEAST threatening to you?

    a. "As a first-time jumper, you may not know the best time to pull the cord."

    b. "As a first-time jumper, you may be so overwhelmed by the experience that you may forget to pull the cord."

    c. "As a first-time jumper, you may have a lot of friends and family watching you from the ground."

The Polar Bear's World

The polar bear is a creature of the ice. Nearly every part of its body is adapted for survival. The bones of the polar bear are filled with an oily marrow that keeps heat in its limbs even in the coldest temperatures. Layers of fat, or blubber, insulate the polar bear, keeping heat from escaping. Other mechanisms the polar bear has for keeping warm are a dark, oily skin that absorbs heat; waterproof fur to keep the bear from getting saturated with icy water; and translucent (see-through) hollow hairs that serve as solar heat conductors.

The polar bear not only has survival mechanisms to stay warm, but also adaptations to help in hunting. The bear's coat color is an array of white and cream, just like the terrain of its habitat, allowing the polar bear to blend right into its surroundings. The only part of the bear's body that is difficult to disguise is its coal-black nose. Polar bears have been known to try hiding their noses by holding their paws over them, pushing ice chunks in front of them, covering them with their tongues, and even packing snow on them to "white them out."

Another hunting advantage the polar bear has is its claws. The polar bear can catch a ringed seal (its favorite food) with just one swipe of its clawed paw. Polar bears use their keen senses of smell and sight to hunt for these seals. Since there is very little vegetation and animal life in the far north, polar bears are constantly in search of food. They take advantage of every opportunity to hunt for seals.

A polar bear may "still hunt," during which the bear waits without moving—sometimes many hours—for a seal to surface for a breath of air. Although polar bears require about one seal per week, they also have the ability to survive on their fat and to eat large quantities of food at one time to be stored as fat.

Since polar bears are always in search of food, they do not have a regular denning or hibernation pattern. On occasion, a polar bear might den for a short period to escape the cold, but the only polar bear that dens for a prolonged period is the pregnant female.

Polar bear cubs are born in litters of two (usually) in a den of ice and snow. They have fur at birth, but they weigh only one and one-half pounds. Although the cubs are born blind and helpless, they weigh 25 pounds by the time they emerge from the den in the spring, and 200 pounds by their first birthday. This is just the start of the cub's growth. Polar bears live about 20 years and grow to weigh between 600 and 1,200 pounds. Cubs stay with their mothers for another one and one-half years after emerging from the den. During this time, they learn how to catch seals.

As soon as the days grow shorter at the end of summer, polar bears gather at the edge of Hudson Bay and other places. When the ice becomes thick enough, hundreds of them venture out on it to catch seals. This practice continues until summer again arrives and the ice breaks up.

In the summer, polar bears eat grass, berries, and seaweed or live off their fat. They amble around, play, and lie on frozen ground to keep cool. If they smell food (such as bacon frying or something roasting), several of them will collect near the enticing smell. The large bears get closest so that if food is given out, they will get it first.

In play, polar bears often face each other, rise, push, shove, and hug each other to keep from falling. They waltz around in the snow. If one topples over, the other immediately throws himself on top and gently bites his opponent.

Occasionally, large males allow cubs to pummel and bite at them. This is a kind of training for the cubs. Mother bears watch carefully so that cubs don't get pushed about too hard.

Mother bears "talk" to their cubs with varying grunts and other sounds. If the cubs are disobedient, the mother bears may cuff them to make them mind.

As the season grows late, the bears assemble at the water's edge. They are hungry and impatient for the ice to become strong enough to support them. Finally, the morning comes when the parade out onto the ice begins.

Read each question. Then circle the letter of the best answer to each question.

1. You want to take a trip to an Arctic region. What information about polar bears WOULD be helpful to know in packing clothes for the trip?

   a. Like a polar bear's skin, dark colors absorb heat rather than reflect it.

   b. Polar bears must constantly search for food because of the poor vegetation in the Arctic regions.

   c. Polar bears have black noses that they often try to cover with their paws or snow.

2. You have a friend who wants to know why polar bears live in such cold climates. Which of the following information would NOT be helpful in your explanation?

   a. Polar bears have many survival mechanisms to help them stay warm.

   b. Polar bears can weigh up to 1,200 pounds.

   c. Polar bears like to eat animals that live in cold climates.

3. You want to gain a better understanding of how polar bears hunt for food. Which experience would NOT be helpful in understanding this?

   a. Interviewing a zoologist who is knowledgeable about polar bears

   b. Viewing a videotape of a female polar bear making a den for her soon-to-arrive cubs

   c. Studying Eskimo art in which polar bear behavior and hunting are shown

4. A friend of yours wants to know how polar bears survive in a land nearly barren of vegetation and animals. Which information would be MOST useful in explaining the bears' survival technique?

   a. Polar bears eat the ringed seal found in the Arctic region.

   b. Pregnant females den for the winter.

   c. Polar bears have the ability to survive on their own fat for a long period without having to eat, and can eat in large quantities at one time if necessary.

5. During your trip to the Arctic Circle, you see some large male polar bears "playing" rather roughly with some polar bear cubs. What information is MOST relevant to understanding this behavior?

   a. Information concerning the temperament of male polar bears

   b. Information concerning the "training" of polar bear cubs in fighting

   c. Information concerning the growth patterns of polar bear cubs

6. A pregnant female polar bear is searching for a good spot to make a den for winter shelter. What information would be MOST pertinent in predicting what spot she will decide on?

   a. Information about the depth of the ice or snow at various spots in the area

   b. Information about the normal number of cubs a polar bear has

   c. Information about the average snowfall that the area receives each year

7. If you wanted to learn how researchers gain information about polar bears, what kind of experience would be MOST helpful?

   a. Visiting an Eskimo village in Alaska where polar bears are often seen

   b. Taking a helicopter ride with a researcher who is tracking a polar bear that is wearing a radio detection device

   c. Taking a commercial tour through Alaska

8. When polar bears know that summer is approaching, they stop hunting for seals and return to land. What information would NOT be relevant to this event?

   a. The amount of daylight is growing shorter each day.

   b. The ice is getting slushy and beginning to break apart.

   c. The temperature is getting warmer.

   d. The bears do not get as hungry as they did at the beginning of the season.

9. Suppose you are a scientist who is studying the polar bears' practice of playing and lying on the ground during the summer months. What information would NOT be useful to you?

   a. Information on how polar bears conserve energy

   b. Information on how polar bears keep cool in the summer

   c. Information on how polar bears nourish their young in the summer

10. When a group of polar bears smells food, the large bears get closest and usually get the food first. What information would be MOST relevant in explaining why this happens?

   a. Information about the role of leadership in a group of polar bears

   b. Information about the digestive system of a polar bear

   c. Information about how polar bears relate to humans

Across the Atlantic in a Sailboat

The need to explore is a characteristic that all humans possess, but some feel more compelled than others to satisfy this need. The Atlantic Ocean has throughout history been a challenge to many explorers. Hanno of Carthage was possibly the first explorer to view the Atlantic Ocean after sailing from the eastern side of the Mediterranean Sea. Many years later a Greek explorer named Pytheas sailed the Atlantic Ocean to find the island that tin came from, now known as Britain.

Other explorers of the Atlantic Ocean were the Vikings from the north in Scandinavia. A Viking by the name of Leif Eriksson is believed to be the first European to have set foot on North American soil. Leif Eriksson and his crew sailed from Greenland to what is now America, but they were frightened by American Indians and decided to return home where they could live peacefully.

Christopher Columbus is more widely considered the "first" to discover America. With three small sailing vessels, Columbus set out to find the Indies in 1492. One month and three days later he found, or thought he found, the Indies. Columbus died before people realized that what he had actually discovered was America.

Since Columbus's voyage, many others have crossed the Atlantic Ocean. Although sailing techniques have changed, the spirit of the explorer is still alive. A modern-day example of this spirit is Gerry Spies,

who crossed the Atlantic in a sailboat. In 1978, Spies finished building the 10-foot *Yankee Girl* in his garage and took it out on White Bear Lake in Minnesota for testing. By July 1, 1979, the boat had been transported to the East Coast and was on its way to England.

Yankee Girl was equipped with sails and a motor. The motor took over at the beginning. The conditions of the first five days permitted Spies to eat only fruit, beef jerky, crackers, and occasionally a peanut butter-and-jelly sandwich. But when the sails were finally up, everything seemed brighter, and Gerry could have hot beef stew.

In the first eight days at sea, Gerry glimpsed the sun but three times, and there were only about 12 hours of favorable winds. On the ninth day, he reached the Gulf Stream, and the next morning he sighted a ship. Gerry was able to talk to the crew and get a message home to his wife, Sally.

Four more days of worsening weather erupted into violence. A 17-foot wave caught Gerry with the hatch cover open. He tumbled into the hold but did not get the cover fastened. Water poured in, and bailing it out was like trying to empty the ocean with a spoon.

The storm subsided, but Gerry's long immersion in salt water removed the top layer of his skin when he changed his clothes. On the 15th day, he had another unexpected dunking. This time he was thrown into the sea when the boat tipped. Luck was with him, however, for another wave righted the boat and deposited him on deck.

The worst of Gerry's problems seemed to be over, and on July 24, he arrived at Falmouth, England, to a huge celebration. This accomplishment didn't satisfy Gerry Spies, however. On July 1, 1981, he and *Yankee Girl* left for Sydney, Australia, where they arrived safely on October 31, 1981.

Read each question. Then circle the letter of the best answer to each question.

1. You must decide when a small sailing vessel should leave port to begin a lengthy ocean voyage. What information would be LEAST relevant to your decision?

   a. The weather conditions at the present time and the forecast for future days

   b. The size of the sailing vessel to be launched

   c. The physical condition of the sailing crew

2. As captain of a small sailing vessel, you must calculate the number of days your voyage will take. Assuming you know the distance of the voyage and the average speed of the vessel, what information would be LEAST relevant to your calculations?

   a. The number of persons sailing on the vessel

   b. The possibility of harsh weather

   c. The prevailing winds in the area through which you will be sailing

3. The number of days that your voyage should take is information that is relevant to . . .

   a. planning the course the vessel will be taking.

   b. planning the amount of food and water needed to survive the voyage.

   c. planning the number of crew members to take on the voyage.

4. Suppose you want to learn the skill of sailing. Which of the following experiences would be LEAST helpful in learning and mastering this skill?

   a. Making a trip to the library to study historical voyages

   b. Talking with experienced sailors and observing them in action

   c. Actual practice sailing a sailboat

   d. Taking a vacation on a large cruise liner

5. In deciding what types of food should be taken on a long sea voyage, which of the following considerations is MOST relevant?

   a. The foods most preferred by the sailors

   b. The amount of space the food takes up

   c. The types of foods that will provide the necessary nutrition for the sailors

   d. How the food is prepared

6. Suppose that when Gerry Spies was thrown into the ocean, he was not washed back on deck, but instead found himself swimming several yards from the boat. Which information would have been MOST useful to Spies in trying to save himself from drowning?

   a. Information concerning the prevailing ocean temperature in which he was located

   b. Information concerning water safety procedures

   c. Information concerning the immediate and future weather conditions

7. Suppose you were in a position to grant money to fund explorations into new areas of knowledge, as was the queen of Spain when Columbus asked her to support his theory of the earth's roundness—an idea that had not yet been supported. What information would be LEAST helpful in making a rational decision about whether to grant the money? (Remember: Columbus's proposal had been refused by one other country—a decision it later regretted.)

   a. The research that the explorer had conducted to prepare for the exploration

   b. The experience and spirit of adventure shown by the explorer

   c. The benefits that your country would reap if the exploration were successful

   d. Your personal opinion about the particular area of knowledge

8. Gerry Spies ate fruit on the first days of his voyage, probably to avoid getting scurvy. Scurvy was first observed by an early explorer who, after running out of fresh fruits and vegetables, noticed his crew suffering from a condition that caused their teeth to fall out. What other information from past explorers would have been helpful for Spies to have learned?

   a. Information about the length of Columbus's journey

   b. Information about the mutiny (rebellion) of the crews of the other sea explorers

   c. Information about how the early explorers recorded their findings on maps

9. Early explorers such as Hanno and Pytheas shared their experiences when they returned home by making books out of the diaries they had kept on their voyages. Which information would NOT be appropriate to include in a diary to be shared with the public?

   a. Information concerning the general health of the captain and crew of the ship

   b. Information concerning the food and water supplies for the captain and crew

   c. Information concerning interesting animals and/or peoples encountered on the voyage

   d. Information concerning the opinion the captain had of his crew

10. Leif Eriksson sailed to America because he was interested in bringing back natural resources not found in Greenland and in finding a good place for his crew to stay for the winter months. As Eriksson and his crew sailed south, they enjoyed the warmer winter and the abundance of trees. Which of the following information was MOST pertinent to Eriksson's departure from America?

   a. The presence of Indians and their culture frightened Eriksson's crew.

   b. The climate in the area (which was probably along the coast of Canada) was unpredictable.

   c. The trees in the area were unfamiliar.

As Warm as Ice

Many people automatically think of the dome-shaped igloo when Eskimos are mentioned. Actually, only eight percent of the total Eskimo population—those who live in the central Arctic region—use igloos as a regular winter dwelling.

Igloos are architecturally sound structures that require considerable skill to build. The biggest problem facing an igloo builder is finding the right kind of snow. The snow must be firm and tightly packed together. It should not be too icy, and it must come from one storm, since snow that has fallen on separate occasions will not hold together well. In the central Arctic region, weather conditions are just right for producing good igloo-building snow. The strong, persistent winds and low temperatures of this region produce the hard, wind-packed snow necessary for igloos. Nowhere else in the world is this type of snow available.

In the past, Eskimos built igloos not only as permanent homes, but also as shelters on hunting trips. An experienced builder could make a warm igloo for two people in 45 minutes.

To make an igloo, the builder cuts snow into blocks and then arranges the blocks in a circle. He works from the inside and makes each circle a little smaller until a dome forms. The builder fills the gaps with snow, cuts a door, then places a block in the doorway to keep out the wind.

Now the house must be "iced." The builder lights a seal-oil lamp. The walls draw the moisture to the outside, where it freezes. Instead of melting the igloo, a small fire or a seal-oil lamp insulates and strengthens it. The builder cuts a hole in the roof and removes the block in the door. As the warm air rushes up, cold air comes in, forming a thin coat of ice on the walls. The structure is now so well insulated that a person can sit inside without wearing a coat, even if the temperature outside drops to –50°F.

Read each question. Then circle the letter of the best answer to each question.

1. You want to learn how to build an igloo. What experience would be MOST helpful in developing this skill?

   a. Learning to fit bricks together in making a brick wall

   b. Going with an Eskimo from the southwestern region of the Arctic to find housing

   c. Visiting a central Arctic Eskimo family while they are moving to a new location during the winter months and therefore planning to prepare appropriate shelter

2. During the process of your igloo training, you must keep a diary of notes so you will be able to recall what you have learned. What information would be MOST relevant for writing in your diary?

    a. The wind conditions on the day you sealed the igloo

    b. The physical characteristics of the snow chosen to make the snow blocks

    c. The date and time of day each step was completed

3. Rather than build igloos, the Eskimos of southwest Alaska dug underground homes, lined them with timber, and covered them with sod. Which information would be relevant in explaining why the Eskimos of the central Arctic did not build structures like these?

    a. The underground structures were unaffected by strong winds.

    b. Timber is impossible to find in the central Arctic region.

    c. Igloos melt each summer, and therefore the Eskimos had to build a new one each year.

4. Even though igloos are used by only eight percent of the total Eskimo population, we often associate the igloo with all Eskimos. Which statement would NOT help explain why this is true?

    a. Homes built underground are not as easily recognized by observers.

    b. Igloos melt each summer, leaving no trace behind.

    c. Architects recognize and often feature igloos as structural masterpieces because they do not have supporting beams.

5. In the central Arctic region, seals are the main source of food for the Eskimos. In addition to using seals for food, Eskimos use seal oil to ice and heat their igloos. Which statement MOST appropriately explains why igloos do not melt when these lamps are used?

    a. Seal-oil lamps are not hot enough to melt an igloo.

    b. The moisture formed on the inside of the walls is drawn outside and refreezes.

    c. Persistent winds keep blowing new snow onto the igloo, thereby replacing the melted areas.

6. From what you read in the article about igloos, which situation would present a serious problem in building an igloo?

   a. A person begins to build an igloo but becomes tired and decides to finish cutting the snow blocks on the following day after a fresh snowfall.

   b. A person has just removed the block from the entrance of the igloo. He or she now will cut a hole in the top of the igloo so that cold air passes through the igloo.

   c. A person has just finished building an igloo and is sitting by a fire he or she has built outside before going inside the igloo for the night's rest.

7. After studying and observing the construction process of an igloo, you plan to make one yourself. Which of the following items would be LEAST appropriate for your task?

   a. A knife strong enough to cut hard-packed snow

   b. A shovel to scoop hard-packed snow into the unfilled cracks of the igloo

   c. A seal-oil lamp to insulate the igloo and make it windproof

8. An Eskimo in the central Arctic region lives in an area that is one of the most difficult in which to survive. What information is MOST convincing in supporting this statement?

   a. Eskimos must build igloos rather than underground shelters.

   b. Extreme temperatures and persistent winds make vegetation in the central Arctic region very scarce.

   c. Eskimos must survive on seals as their main source of nourishment and fuel.

9. Eskimos in the central Arctic region felt that igloos were superior to underground houses. What information is NOT relevant to this point of view?

   a. Information concerning the number of years a person could dwell in a single underground home

   b. Information concerning the mobility central Arctic Eskimos needed in their hunt for food

   c. Information concerning the amount of time it took to build an igloo

10. You must decide when an Eskimo should go on a lengthy hunting trip for seals (an igloo would need to be built). What information would be LEAST relevant to your decision?

   a. Information concerning the present food supply

   b. Information concerning the present supply of seal oil

   c. Information concerning the supply of sealskins

Message in a Bottle

Ake was a sailor on a Swedish ship in 1956. He found the long hours at sea boring, and he longed for a wife and a chance to settle down. In desperation, he wrote a message, sealed it in a bottle, and dropped it into the ocean. The message asked any pretty girl who found the bottle to write to him. Two years later, Ake received a reply.

A Sicilian fisherman had found Ake's bottle and given the message to his daughter, Paulina. She, in turn, had sent greetings to Ake. A short time later, Ake visited Sicily. The friendship grew, and he and Paulina were married in the fall of 1958. Ake didn't have a computer, but he still found a wife half a world away.

Even though bottles seem fragile, they can last for many years at sea. One of the most unusual cases was that of Chinosuke Matsuyama, a Japanese seaman. He and his companions were shipwrecked on a Pacific coral reef. Before he died of starvation, he carved a brief report of their ordeal in 1784 on a piece of wood, sealed it in a bottle, and threw it into the sea. The bottle washed ashore 150 years later, next to the village where Matsuyama had been born.

A group of German scientists are probably the champions in the race for the longest bottle voyage on record. These oceanographers (scientists who study the ocean) were part of an expedition to the Indian Ocean in 1929. They designed a bottle with a message that could be read without opening or breaking the bottle. The message asked the finder to report where he or she had found it and to throw it back into the sea. The bottle floated eastward to South America, where people all along the west coast reported it. It then made its way back to the Indian Ocean and southward to Australia. Six years elapsed, and during that period, winds and ocean currents had carried the bottle more than 16,000 miles. That is more than six miles a day.

Bottles have also been used to carry secret messages. In 1875, the crew of the small Canadian ship *Lennie* mutinied in the English Channel and killed the ship's officers. The steward who served the food aboard the *Lennie* was spared because he knew how to navigate (steer) the ship. The steward sailed the ship secretly toward the French coast and dropped several bottles overboard that contained messages describing what had happened. French police found one of the bottles, read the message, boarded the ship, and arrested the astonished crew.

Benjamin Franklin was among the first to recognize the usefulness of bottles in charting ocean currents. He knew that Colonial whaling ships crossed the Atlantic much more rapidly than British mail carriers. So when he became postmaster general for the colonies, he interviewed the whaling captains and began dropping bottles into the Gulf Stream. He asked those who found the bottles to notify him. His technique for charting ocean currents is still used today to predict the movements of oil slicks, sea mines, and even schools of fish.

Read each question. Then circle the best answer to each question below.

1. You are interested in knowing how far a bottle has traveled. What would be the MOST relevant information to secure?

    a. The date on which the bottle was released

    b. The place at which the bottle was released

    c. The size of the bottle that was released

2. You are interested in knowing why the bottle was released. What would be the MOST relevant information to secure?

    a. The date on which the bottle was released

    b. The place at which the bottle was released

    c. The information requested on the note inside the bottle

3. You are interested in knowing where a bottle was released. What is the MOST relevant information to secure?

    a. The type of glass that was used in making the bottle

    b. Information on the winds and tide during the two-week voyage of the bottle

    c. The information requested on the note inside the bottle

4. If you hope to receive a response from a note you will send in a bottle, what would be the MOST relevant information to send?

    a. Information on the type of work you do

    b. Your address and phone number

    c. A description of your family

5. You have found a bottle with U.S. government markings on it but no address. What would be the MOST relevant information for you to have?

    a. Information about governmental agencies that help the fishing industry

    b. Information about governmental agencies that use bottles to collect information

    c. A chart showing the location of lighthouses

6. You have found a bottle with a note written in a foreign language. Where would be the MOST relevant place to seek assistance?

   a. A minister, priest, or rabbi

   b. A foreign language department at a university

   c. A code-breaking expert with the F.B.I.

7. You want to find a very strong bottle to send a message. Where would be the MOST relevant place to seek assistance?

   a. A storekeeper who keeps bottles of food

   b. A friend who stores coins and buttons in jars

   c. A glass-bottle manufacturing company

8. You are hoping to find a bottle with a message. What would be the MOST relevant or appropriate time to search for a bottle?

   a. When the wind and tide are coming toward the shore

   b. When the tide is going out

   c. When a violent storm is raging

9. You are shipwrecked and trying to send for help using a bottle. What would be the MOST relevant information to put in the message?

   a. How many people there are in your party

   b. How much food you have left

   c. Where you are located

10. Benjamin Franklin was trying to determine which ships crossed the Atlantic Ocean the fastest. What information was the MOST relevant in his search for answers?

   a. Knowing which ships had the most sails

   b. Knowing when ships left port and arrived

   c. Knowing which ships were the largest

The Amazing Dolphins

Dolphins are small, toothed whales that belong to the mammal classification of animals. This means that dolphins have mammary glands that produce milk for their young. Mammals also have lungs, breathe oxygen, and are warm-blooded.

Dolphins have many interesting characteristics. They use blowholes on the top of their heads to breathe. Dolphins can rest for several hours on the top of the water using their top fins for balance and their blowholes for breathing. While under the water, dolphins cover their blowholes. When a dolphin is born, its mother must push it to the surface of the water for its first breath.

Although the blowhole is a characteristic similar to a human nose, it does not have the ability to smell. Dolphins have no sense of smell and very little sense of taste. This may be why they swallow their food whole. Dolphins have a keen sense of hearing, however. They locate objects in the water by making clicking noises and listening for those sounds to reflect, or echo, off the object.

Dolphins swim together in groups called pods, enabling them to hunt together and protect each other from danger. One way dolphins protect each other is by slapping their tail fins, or flukes, against the surface of the water to warn the pod of a nearby enemy. Common enemies of a pod of dolphins are tiger sharks and killer whales.

Another problem for dolphins is shallow waters. When a dolphin finds itself in water that is not deep enough, it may become stranded on the shore. The dolphin's skin may then dry out, causing the animal to overheat and die.

In December 1983, two people at a beach in Provincetown, Massachusetts, heard a high-pitched whistle, then saw a lone dolphin stranded in shallow water. They rushed to call the Center for Coastal Studies a few miles away. The Northeast Stranding Network went quickly into action. These rescuers slipped a tarp under the struggling animal. The outlook for saving the dolphin was slim. No deep-sea dolphin had ever been successfully restored to its native waters.

By 6 P.M., the Mystic Marinelife Aquarium had a van equipped with a stretcher, water sprayers, insulated ice containers, and Crisco (to keep the dolphin's delicate skin from tearing) at the Provincetown beach. When the dolphin arrived at the aquarium, the staff was ready for 24-hour watches. The 6-foot, 280-pound, male black-and-white dolphin was offered a herring laced with antibiotic and also live trout. He was not interested, so staff members opened his mouth and put the herring in.

On the second night of the around-the-clock vigil, the dolphin made a dash for the side of the pool and rammed into the concrete, breaking his jaw. Now the jaw had to be wedged open in order to heal. He was dubbed "Harvey Wallbanger."

By the end of the month, Harvey was improving. He was gulping 14 pounds of herring a day. He became playful, darting around staffers and stopping for hugs. Near the end of March, a fishing captain called to say he had sighted a pod of white-siders (like Harvey).

On April 11, Harvey was loaded up and taken to sea. The pod was located, and Harvey was slid into the ocean. At first the pod circled. Then one dolphin broke away and came to Harvey, and soon others followed. Harvey had made it!

Read each question. Then circle the letter of the best answer to each question.

1. You must attempt to rescue a stranded dolphin. Which information would be the LEAST helpful in determining the first steps to take?

   a. The condition of the dolphin's skin

   b. Rescue methods that have been successful in the past

   c. The age of the stranded dolphin

2. This selection considers the slim chances of saving a stranded dolphin. What information would be the LEAST useful in determining the chances of a dolphin's successful return to the sea?

   a. Information concerning previous attempts to return a stranded dolphin to its natural habitat

   b. Information about a dolphin's normal behavior and eating habits

   c. Information concerning the dolphin's general health

   d. Information concerning the migration of dolphin pods

3. Which event is the MOST relevant to Harvey's final return to native waters?

   a. A fishing captain had sighted a pod of white-siders.

   b. The pod of dolphins circled around Harvey.

   c. One dolphin broke away from the pod to join Harvey.

4. Based on the information in this story, you might conclude that dolphins are friendly creatures. Which item is MOST relevant to this conclusion?

   a. Once Harvey began to recover, he became playful, darting around staffers and stopping for hugs.

   b. A pod of white-sided dolphins had been sighted by a local fishing captain.

   c. The pod of dolphins circled as Harvey was placed back into the ocean.

5. You are asked to make a list of the characteristics that qualify dolphins as mammals. Which information would NOT be helpful for this list?

   a. Dolphins have delicate skin.

   b. Baby dolphins feed on their mothers' milk.

   c. Dolphins breathe oxygen and have lungs.

6. Assume you are a dolphin swimming with your pod. You hear one of the other dolphins in your pod slapping the surface of the water with its flukes. Which of the following reactions would be fitting?

   a. Begin swimming with the pod to the food supply that has been located

   b. Begin swimming with the pod away from the enemy that has been located

   c. Begin swimming with the pod away from the shallow waters that are nearby

7. Suppose that one of the dolphins in a pod is wounded by an enemy. Based on what you have read, which of the following would be an appropriate prediction of what might happen?

   a. The rest of the dolphins would quickly separate and find their own safety.

   b. The rest of the dolphins would signal danger and swim away together.

   c. The rest of the dolphins would signal danger and stay to protect the wounded dolphin.

8. If you were ever to care for a stranded dolphin, what information would be the MOST helpful in keeping the dolphin from harming itself as did Harvey?

    a. Dolphins are not used to swimming in confined areas.

    b. Dolphins are playful, friendly creatures.

    c. Dolphins breathe oxygen and have lungs.

9. Which information would be MOST pertinent in understanding why dolphins swim in pods?

    a. Information concerning the life spans of dolphins

    b. Information concerning the methods of protection used by pods of dolphins

    c. Information concerning the growth of the pod

10. Suppose you develop an interest in dolphins and visit the Sea World dolphin area to learn more about the animal. The trainer suggests that you observe some of the dolphins before she or he speaks with you about any questions you might have. Which of the following types of information would be LEAST helpful in enhancing your observation?

    a. Information explaining how dolphins breathe

    b. Information about the sensory organs of dolphins

    c. Information about the functions of the body parts of a dolphin

    d. Information about the trainer's experience with training dolphins

II.

Just the Facts, Ma'am:

Distinguishing Among Facts, Assumptions, and Values

Introduction

Facts and Assumptions

If you have ever watched a detective show on television or followed a trial in the news, you know the importance of "getting the facts." Detectives can't arrest a person simply because they think the individual *looks* guilty, and a jury can't convict a defendant simply because the person *seems* to have committed a crime. Law enforcement officers and legal guardians search for documented evidence and established facts. They have to prove that the defendant is guilty beyond a reasonable doubt. They want and need *facts,* not assumptions and opinions.

Facts are directly tied to proof. You may hear all kinds of stories at school and in your neighborhood. These are not facts. They are simply rumors until they are established as true. Your friends probably hold very different views regarding clothing styles, food preferences, and hobbies. These views are not facts, either; they are opinions. A fact is a statement about a person, an object, or an event that has been verified and documented. It has been observed, usually by several persons, and proved to be true through the use of accepted methods of examination and inquiry.

We frequently hear people say that they have the *true* facts or the *real* facts, even though one fact cannot be truer or more real than any other fact. Either it is a fact or it isn't—facts are not graded or ranked in quality.

However, some facts (like the number of bushels of corn grown in a year) may change over time.

If we have a strong belief that certain information is factual but we have no proof, we can make a careful guess. This guess is called an *assumption.* We cannot call our assumption a fact until we have documented proof that our assumption is correct.

It is sometimes tempting to make big assumptions based on small facts—but the wisest people stay close to the facts at hand and make no claims beyond what they know to be true. Consider the story about President Eliot of Harvard University and a hat-check girl in New York City. President Eliot gave his hat to the hat-check girl as he entered a restaurant. After dinner, the girl retrieved his hat from a large shelf on which 50 hats were stored. "How did you know that was my hat?" the president asked. The girl replied, "I didn't, sir." "Then why did you give it to me?" Eliot asked. "Because you gave it to me, sir," was the girl's reply. President Eliot was impressed with the hat-check girl's careful concern for accuracy. She did not go beyond what she knew about the hat. She made no assumptions.

It is also important to recognize the difference between *personal* and *public* knowledge. When a friend tells you about her dreams or her feelings about a classmate, there is no way that you can observe these experiences directly. These dreams or feelings are your friend's personal knowledge. On the other hand, there are many events that can be observed by more than one person. This is public knowledge. If your brother tells you that there is a penguin in the refrigerator, you can go check for yourself. We become more confident about our observations when they are checked by others.

Four events are described below. Which two depend most upon *personal* knowledge?

1. Jack felt his confidence slipping away as the opposing team's score passed 100.

2. Bill and Tom could not get Bob's car started.

3. Tod sensed danger as he walked into the gloomy house.

4. Sally screamed when she and her friends saw the dead snake in her locker.

Did you choose number 1 and number 3? Jack and Tod had experiences that they could share only indirectly with others. They were internal feelings. Sally also had internal feelings about the snake, but her scream and the presence of her friends at the event made it public. Bill and Tom's problem starting the car could also be observed directly.

Values

What are values? Are they real or simply figments of our imaginations? Values are not real in the sense that we can see or touch them, yet they are certainly real in the way they affect our lives. It is fascinating to trace the life stories of people who often drifted aimlessly before they clarified their values.

One young French lad did little but fish and loaf around town until his late 20s. Another, a German youth, spent most of his first 30 years fighting, chasing girls, and getting drunk. Still another young man of Jewish parentage couldn't speak a word until he was 3 and found only ill-paying, grubby

office jobs until he was in his middle 20s. Each had a rather forlorn beginning, yet eventually they became known to the world as Louis Pasteur, Otto von Bismarck, and Albert Einstein, respectively. The turning points in each of their lives were marked by the crystallizing of clear, meaningful life goals.

It is hard to imagine a world without values, for our values provide the very foundation on which we consciously or unconsciously make decisions about our daily activities. What we choose to do with our time, how we spend our money, what we establish as life goals, and whom we choose to be with all depend upon the values we have accepted or developed on our own. Indeed, values are so important to us that without some sense of purpose or direction we would become mentally ill. Our personal values supply us with three essentials: (1) a sense of purpose; (2) guidelines for the conduct of the groups we belong to; and (3) a code for judging right from wrong, fair from unfair, and moral behavior from immoral behavior.

The words *should* and *ought* are often found in value statements. These words suggest that a person has an obligation or a duty, and they also indicate that things would be better if certain kinds of actions were either supported or avoided. The statement "Tom *ought* to help the team" implies that Tom has some obligation to the team and that the team would be better with his help.

Values don't occur as spur-of-the-moment hunches, preferences, or fads. They are ideas that we consider desirable, good, and just. In many cases, we must set aside our own selfish desires to promote values that are beneficial to others as well as ourselves.

Use the following summary to help you distinguish among facts, assumptions, and values.

1. We are all exposed to a great deal of information in our lives. Some of this information is little more than rumor or opinion. We do, however, have hunches from day to day about what we think is true. We call these hunches *assumptions.* Assumptions are not factual until they have been proved to be true through careful observation, usually by several persons. They then become *facts.*

2. *Personal* knowledge is very different from *public* knowledge. In most instances, we cannot examine and verify personal knowledge in the same way we can document and prove public knowledge and information.

3. *Values* are very different from facts and assumptions. Values are ideas, traditions, and patterns of behavior that we consider very important, desirable, and worthwhile. They are ideals that we cherish, support, and defend.

Read the sentences below. Categorize each statement by writing *fact, assumption,* or *value statement* in the blank. Remember, facts can be observed and proved, assumptions deal with hunches, and value statements tell what people consider important and desirable.

_____   1. George left by train at 4 P.M.

_____   2. Ruth expects camp to be fun.

_____   3. Ramón believes that patriotism ought to be stressed.

_____   4. Jesse lost his ring during the game.

_____   5. Albert thinks the team will win the play-offs.

_____   6. Rubin is six feet tall.

_____   7. Sandra believes that we should welcome new people to the club.

_____   8. Tim thinks eighth grade will be more difficult than seventh.

_____   9. Alex thinks we ought to stress our family traditions.

_____   10. Football players at the high school practice 14 hours a week.

In the following exercises, you will be asked to distinguish among facts, assumptions, and values.

Who Has the Right to Decide?

Who should decide how a sick or disabled child should be cared for: the parents or health authorities? After Juliet Cheng immigrated to the United States from China a decade ago, she had a daughter she named Shirley. When Shirley was 11 months old, she was diagnosed as having a crippling joint disease. Cheng first turned to an American doctor. He prescribed aspirin to ease the pain and swelling in the baby's joints.

When the aspirin didn't help, Cheng treated her daughter at home with herbal potions. She also took her back to China, where Shirley was treated with acupuncture, massage, and medicines made from animal glands. Cheng believed that she could see real improvement in her daughter's condition, so she made three additional trips to China for treatments.

Shirley suffered a relapse after returning from her last trip to China, and a doctor in her hometown recommended that Mrs. Cheng consult a specialist at a children's hospital.

Doctors at the hospital told Mrs. Cheng that Shirley would never walk again unless she had surgery to relieve the tightness in the tendons and ligaments around the joints in her hips, knees, and left ankle.

Mrs. Cheng refused to allow the surgery, and the hospital persuaded the state Department of Children and Youth Services to go to court so that the state could take custody of Shirley. The judge decided to give Mrs. Cheng two months to prove that non-Western treatments of the joint disease could help her daughter.

Issues of parental rights and children's health are not simple. The United States Supreme Court ruled recently that lower courts were correct in requiring a Laotian family to submit their child for surgery even though it was against their beliefs. The hospital where the surgery was to be performed, however, refused to do the operation without the consent of the parents. Hospitals generally require parental permission before surgery.

In the blank beside each statement, write *fact, assumption,* or *value statement.*

_____ 1. Juliet Cheng immigrated to the United States from China.

_____ 2. Aspirin didn't help Shirley.

_____ 3. We should have a right to select our own medical treatments.

36

_____   4. Mrs. Cheng refused to allow surgery.

_____   5. We ought to have faith in the use of natural medicines.

_____   6. We should realize that Chinese medicine has important strengths.

7. Which of the following value statements is clearly reflected in the judge's decision regarding Mrs. Cheng's case? Put a check mark beside the best answer.

_____ a. People should have an opportunity to prove that they are right.

_____ b. We should recognize that medical doctors know best.

_____ c. Mothers should make decisions regarding a child's treatment.

_____ d. The child herself should make the decision regarding treatment.

_____ e. The courts should have no say in matters of this kind.

_____ f. We must recognize that no medical care is better than the wrong care.

8. Why did you select the value statement you chose for number 7?

_____

_____

_____

9. Which of the following value statements is clearly reflected in the United States Supreme Court ruling? Put a check mark beside the best answer.

_____ a. The parent should decide what's best for the child.

_____ b. Hospitals should decide whether to perform surgery.

_____ c. Parents should be required to provide proper medical care.

_____ d. Cultural traditions should be respected.

_____ e. Medical services are not an issue that should concern the courts.

_____ f. Natural healing powers are most important.

10. Why did you select the value statement you chose for number 9?

_____

_____

_____

Strange Ways of Predicting the Future

In 1796, a group of worried generals crowded around a table in a secret military headquarters hidden in the forests of eastern Austria. They were carefully following the movements of a tiny mouse on a military map. The feet of the mouse had been dipped in ink so that every movement of its feet made marks on the chart. This was not just a game. The generals believed that the frightened mouse could somehow help them find an escape route from Napoleon's advancing armies. The bewildered mouse's tracks proved to be useless, however, and the Austrian armies were quickly defeated.

People everywhere from the very early days to the present have wanted to predict the future. If we knew today what was going to happen in the days ahead, we might be able to avoid disasters and plan our lives more carefully. The early Greeks went to a temple called Delphi where a woman in a trance would utter weird sounds. The priests at the temple would then explain what the sounds meant. Many of the early Greeks believed that Apollo, the god of light and purity, predicted the future directly through the garbled sounds of the oracle's voice.

Even today, people search for clues to the future by consulting horoscopes and reading tarot cards. Eighty million Americans read their horoscopes every day. Some of these readers are seriously trying to predict their own futures; others are curious or amused by the descriptions.

Horoscopes supposedly show the positions of the stars at the time of a person's birth. The stars are believed to influence the character of the person. Some also believe that horoscopes may predict impending events.

Tarot cards are consulted much like horoscopes. There are 78 elaborately decorated cards in a tarot deck. They feature cups, coins, swords, and staffs. It is believed that these objects at one time represented four classes of medieval society: cups for the clergy, coins for the merchants, swords for the nobility, and staffs for the peasants. Each time a person inquires about his future, the cards are placed facedown in a pattern known as the *Tree of Life*. As each card is turned faceup, the symbols are interpreted. The symbols may predict long life and happiness or, perhaps, hidden enemies and suffering.

Birds have often been used to predict the future. When planning a voyage or a military campaign, the ancient Greeks would often draw a circle and divide it into 24 sections. Each section contained a kernel of corn and a letter of the Greek alphabet. A small rooster was then placed in the circle. The order in which he picked up the corn spelled out a message from the gods. Birds are also used to predict the future in China today. A fortune-teller prepares a small cage with tiny birds inside and a set of cards held upright in a wooden card-holder. When a person inquires about his future, the fortune-teller opens the cage door. A bird hops out and picks up a card in its beak. The card supposedly helps answer the visitor's questions about his future.

Water has been used almost as frequently as birds to forecast the future and to decide the guilt or innocence of prisoners. In early settlements in what is now the United States, women who were thought to be witches were tied up and thrown into a river or pond. Judges at that time thought that water would reject a child of Satan. If the unfortunate woman sank, she was quickly rescued. If she did not sink, she was put to death. Water has also been used to read romantic futures. Girls would write the names of their boyfriends on separate pieces of paper and drop them into a bathtub of water. These girls believed that the name that rose and floated first held the name of their future husband.

Many years ago, parents of very young children in Europe tried to discover what kinds of talents their offspring might have. After the child learned to crawl, the parents would place a violin, a carpenter's saw, and a farmer's sickle on the floor near the child. The parents believed that the child would reveal his future life's work by grabbing the object that matched his talents.

I. In the blank beside each statement, write *fact, assumption,* or *value statement.*

_____ 1. European parents wanted to identify their children's talents.

_____ 2. European parents should have waited until later in the child's life.

_____ 3. It might be helpful to know about children's talents very early in their lives.

_____ 4. The child had only three choices.

_____ 5. Parents today ought to try this technique to see if it works.

_____ 6. The European parents did not really think this technique would work.

_____ 7. We ought to be exploring new ways of identifying children's talents.

II. Which of the following value statements is not reflected in the treatment of accused witches in the article? Put a check mark beside the correct answer.

_____ a. Witches should be protected.

_____ b. Witches ought to be identified and punished.

_____ c. Witches should be seen as children of Satan.

_____ d. If a woman sinks below the surface of the water, she should be saved.

_____   e. Witches should not be allowed to live.

_____   f. Witches ought to be seen as a menace to society.

_____   g. A witch should not be granted forgiveness.

III. Why did you select the value statement you chose?

_____

_____

_____

_____

IV. In the blank beside each statement, write *fact, assumption,* or *value statement.*

_____   1. Birds may be used to predict the future because people have been amazed at their ability to fly.

_____   2. Birds should not be expected to predict future events.

_____   3. The brains of birds are very small.

_____   4. Birds should be allowed to fly freely. They should not be kept in cages.

_____   5. If the birds' predictions were always wrong, you would think that customers would not return to the fortune-teller.

_____   6. People who use birds to make predictions may believe that mysterious forces guide the birds.

_____   7. Birds spend a lot of time looking for food.

V. Why do you think people are so curious about what will happen to them in the future? Write your answer on the lines below.

_____

_____

_____

To the North Pole

From the time he was a very young man, Robert Peary was determined to be the first person to reach the North Pole. It took him 20 years to realize his goal.

Peary first entered the navy and became a naval officer. He recognized that his goal of reaching the North Pole would require sophisticated navigational skills and thoughtful planning. His eventual success was due to careful preparation as well as enormous personal determination.

Peary participated in several Arctic expeditions to find out as much as he could about surviving in the Arctic cold. During these expeditions, he learned a great deal about travel in the bleak, forbidding areas of the North. He developed a number of new methods of fighting the winter winds. This new knowledge helped him reach his ultimate goal.

From every failure, Peary learned something that would eventually lead to success. He found out how to sail through and around drifting ice. He spent years exploring Greenland to find the best spot for his final push to the Pole. He also learned how to help his men preserve their strength in the frigid reaches of the Arctic Circle. He developed better ways of caring for the dogs that pulled the sleds and the supplies.

Peary's main assistant was Matthew Henson, a black man and the only American in his expedition. Henson built specially designed sleds and learned to speak the Eskimo language. He was also an experienced navigator who knew the tides and ice packs. Henson was an expert handler of sled dogs. He could avoid crevasses and gauge the thickness of the ice. Henson saved Peary's life on several occasions.

Henson was as determined to reach the pole as Peary was. He taught members of the expedition how to brave the hazards of frigid weather and long periods of isolation. Finally, on April 6, 1909, Peary and Henson stood at the top of the world, the first explorers to reach the North Pole.

In the blank beside each statement, write *fact, assumption,* or *value statement.*

_____   1. It took Peary 20 years to reach his goal.

_____   2. Peary first entered the navy and became a naval officer.

_____   3. We must recognize that reaching the Pole was worthwhile.

_____   4. Peary spent years exploring Greenland.

_____   5. If Henson hadn't been there, Peary wouldn't have succeeded.

_____   6. Determination like Peary's is very important.

_____   7. If Peary were alive today, he would be interested in space exploration.

8. Which of the following value statements is NOT reflected in Peary's effort to reach the Pole? Put a check mark beside the best answer.

_____   a. Determination is an important factor in achievement.

_____   b. Careful planning is crucial to such an expedition.

_____   c. Cooperation among members is very important.

_____   d. The protection of penguins should help bring final success.

_____   e. The development of new types of equipment should be stressed.

_____   f. Dogs should be cared for attentively.

_____   g. Advanced navigational skills should be emphasized.

9. Why did you select the value statement you chose for question 8?

_____

_____

_____

_____

10. If you were interviewing a person who wanted to join your expedition, how would you rate the importance of the following values he or she held? Put a 1 beside the most important, a 2 beside the next most important, and so on, until you rate all seven.

_____　a. He or she values cleanliness.

_____　b. He or she values body strength and conditioning.

_____　c. He or she feels that careful preparation is important.

_____　d. He or she feels that cooperation is crucial.

_____　e. He or she believes in saving money.

_____　f. He or she has a strong belief in perseverance.

_____　g. He or she is a good photographer who values great pictures.

11. Why did you select your first choice for number 10?

_____

_____

_____

12. Why did you select your last choice for number 10?

_____

_____

_____

Chief of the Eel River Tribes

His name was *Me-she-kin-no-quah,* which white men translated as "Little Turtle." He was chief of the Eel River Miami, an American Indian tribe. Many historians consider him the greatest American Indian who ever lived. He was a brave soldier, a brilliant strategist, and a wise leader. Unfortunately, he lived during a time of great conflict. Little Turtle and his warriors, armed with rifles, normally sided with the British in the French and British struggle for control of the lands south of the Great Lakes.

Early in Little Turtle's career as chief, a dashing French soldier of fortune, Augustin Mottin de la Balme, sought to conquer the region. Fortunately, Little Turtle had a plan. Otherwise, the course of the American Revolution as well as the War of 1812 might have been irreversibly changed. La Balme was inspired by George Rogers Clark's success at Vincennes, and he developed a bold strategy to take Detroit from the British. Gathering a small army of Frenchmen, he started north in 1780, pausing briefly to destroy the key Miami village of Kekionga, where Fort Wayne, Indiana, now stands. Encouraged by the Kekionga victory and believing that he had the Miami on the run, La Balme decided to replenish his supplies of food and ammunition by raiding a British trading post on the Eel River. He turned in that direction and set up camp for the night. Little Turtle silently encircled La Balme's army, and before the light of dawn the next morning, he fell upon the sleeping soldiers. Only one captive lived to tell the story.

This astonishing victory lifted Little Turtle into the highest ranks of his people and gained him greater respect among the British. At this point, the upper Eel River area was firmly in the grasp of Little Turtle, and the victorious chief returned to his village near the center of the region. Peace lasted for more than 10 years, but a new and greater threat soon appeared. Alarmed by clashes on the frontier, the federal government in Philadelphia ordered General Josiah Harmar, Commander in Chief of the Army, to take charge of the American Indians.

Harmar was authorized to recruit 1,500 men. When he arrived at Kekionga, he found the village deserted. Believing that the Miami had fled, the general sent Colonel Hardin with 210 men out to destroy them. Little Turtle, who knew the region like the palm of his hand, hastily pulled together 300 warriors and headed for a marshy area. He hid his men among the trees. Believing that the Miami would not attack a force as strong as his, Hardin marched his men into the middle of the swamp. At a preplanned moment, the Miami opened fire and advanced along the paths that they had long used through the marsh. Most of the soldiers fled, and the few that stood and fought were killed. Little Turtle then followed this success with another victory over General Harmar's forces.

There was great despair in Philadelphia. The next year, General James

Wilkinson was sent to the region to raid the villages of the Miami Indians. He destroyed a village at Kenapacomaqua in what is now known as the Battle of Old Towne. Wilkinson escaped the forces of Little Turtle, who was waiting for a larger group of American infantry nearby. The chief routed the larger American force led by General Arthur St. Clair and in doing so killed or wounded almost two thirds of the army.

Three years later, George Washington sent General "Mad" Anthony Wayne to subdue the Miami. Little Turtle urged his people to quit the fight. He pointed out that General Wayne was a chief who never slept. Despite the greatest planning, the Miami were never able to surprise him. Little Turtle's fellow chiefs accused him of cowardice and chose a new leader, Blue Jacket, to take his place.

Shortly thereafter, the Miami were defeated at the Battle of Fallen Timbers. Too late, the other chiefs recognized the wisdom of Little Turtle's counsel. The Miami signed a treaty giving up two thirds of Ohio and part of southeastern Indiana. As he signed the treaty, Little Turtle said, "I am the last to sign this treaty, and I will be the last to break it." He never did.

General Wayne was impressed with Little Turtle's dignity and competence. He urged the chief to visit President Washington in Philadelphia. When Little Turtle visited, Washington gave him a sword and a peace medal. Washington commissioned Gilbert Stuart, a famous portrait painter, to paint his picture. Little Turtle was later received by John Adams and Thomas Jefferson.

Little Turtle was more than a wartime leader. He recognized the problems that liquor caused among the Miami. He addressed Congress in his fight to ban alcohol from his tribe. The chief also recognized the importance of health. At that time, vaccinations were just being introduced. Little Turtle was not only vaccinated himself, but he also took vaccine back to his people.

Little Turtle realized that his people could no longer live by hunting. He persuaded the Quakers of Baltimore to send a teacher of agriculture to instruct his people in farming. In addition, he persuaded Congress to appropriate $15,000 toward the teacher's support. It was a difficult but wise decision. Courageous in war and wise in peace, Little Turtle died in 1812, justly honored by white people and American Indians alike.

In the blank beside each statement, write *fact, assumption,* or *value statement.*

_____ 1. Little Turtle was chief of the Eel River Miami.

_____ 2. Little Turtle should be recognized as the greatest American Indian.

_____ 3. If Blue Jacket had been successful, he would have been chief for the rest of his life.

_____ 4. We must send our greatest generals into battle, because American lives are as important as victory.

_____ 5. We should vaccinate for the protection of our health.

_____   6. Little Turtle was honored by both American
                                      Indians and white people.

_____   7. If Little Turtle were alive today, he could
                                      really help American Indians.

8. It is obvious that Little Turtle changed a great deal from his early years as a warrior to the end of his life. Which of the following values did his activities reflect at the beginning of his career? Put a check mark beside the FOUR best answers.

_____   a. People should protect their home territories.

_____   b. Bravery and cunning are important.

_____   c. We should not kill animals.

_____   d. Tricking the enemy is justified in times of war.

_____   e. American Indians should not own guns.

_____   f. White people should not be killed.

_____   g. It is wise to watch for dangers.

9. Which of the following values did his activities reflect near the close of his life? Put a check mark beside the FOUR best answers.

_____   a. American Indians should make peace with white people.

_____   b. All people should be concerned with good health.

_____   c. When conditions change, we should seek help from former enemies and change ourselves.

_____   d. We should realize that old habits and traditions are best.

_____   e. American Indians should not mingle with white people.

_____   f. Enemies should be enemies forever.

_____   g. We should not fight battles we can't win.

10. Why did you check *c* in the list above?

_____

_____

_____

Caring for Our Animal Friends

Every year hundreds of thousands of cats and dogs are destroyed by animal pounds throughout the United States. These frightened, homeless creatures are the victims of thoughtless people who cannot or will not care for them. In many instances, unwanted kittens and puppies are born and purposely drowned or abandoned in fields and wooded areas beyond city limits. If the abandoned creatures do not die on the highways or from starvation, they are picked up and taken to research laboratories for medical experiments or to animal shelters where they are held for short periods of time and then put to death.

Even if the stray dogs and cats manage to evade capture, they are likely to suffer from the effects of malnutrition, disease, and frigid weather. Without shots and preventive medications, they are vulnerable to a number of serious diseases, including mange, hookworm, distemper, rabies, and heartworm. In addition, they are likely to reproduce and start the whole cycle of suffering over again for their offspring. As the numbers of unwanted animals mount, Humane Society officials are increasingly overwhelmed with the task of caring for these needy creatures.

Some zoologists and animal-management specialists believe that people should not interfere with nature, particularly the laws of natural selection. They believe that when the strongest and fittest and cleverest members of a species survive, and the weaker and less clever die off, the species is strengthened. They point out, for example, that when we vaccinate animals against diseases, we are interfering with their own natural defenses, called antibodies. In time, their natural immunities may be lost altogether. What appears to be kindness is, in the long run, a shortsighted disservice to the animals themselves.

In the blank beside each statement, write *fact, assumption,* or *value statement.*

_____

1. Hundreds of thousands of cats and dogs are destroyed each year.

_____

2. We must learn to deal with this problem more intelligently.

_____

3. We should not interfere with the laws of nature.

_____

4. Humane Society officials are increasingly overwhelmed.

_____   5. Animals often die on highways.

_____   6. If people watched for stray animals, we could eliminate the problem.

_____   7. If animal-management specialists and Humane Society officials could agree, we could help thousands of suffering animals.

8. Humane Society officials and animal-management specialists hold different views regarding stray animals. Which of the following value statements are reflected in the position taken by Humane Society officials? Put a check mark beside the TWO best answers.

_____   a. We ought to provide help for stray animals.

_____   b. Animals should not depend on people for care.

_____   c. Animals should be given proper medical care.

_____   d. We should realize that big dogs belong in the country.

_____   e. Cats are not friendly toward people, and we should not be as concerned with them as we are with dogs.

_____   f. We shouldn't feed stray animals.

_____   g. The problem of stray animals should eventually cure itself.

9. Which of the following value statements are clearly reflected in the position taken by animal-management specialists? Put a check mark beside the FIVE best answers.

_____   a. We should not interfere with nature and the survival of the fittest.

_____   b. We must not weaken an animal's natural defenses against disease.

_____   c. It is good for the species if weaker and less clever animals die off.

_____   d. We should provide help for stray animals.

_____   e. All stray animals should be given proper medical care.

_____   f. We should recognize that kindness may be shortsighted.

_____   g. We should recognize that we simply can't deal adequately with so many stray animals.

10. Why did you not put a check mark beside *e* in the list above?

_____

_____

_____

She Chose Freedom

Harriet Tubman was born into slavery in 1820 or 1821 on a farm in Dorchester County, Maryland. She was put to work before she was six years old as a babysitter for children of white landowners. It was a difficult job because if the baby cried, Harriet was whipped. At an age when she would normally have been in kindergarten, she had already been given responsibilities typically assigned to adults. Harriet was one of 11 children, so she had seen children cared for at home. Nevertheless, it was a very large responsibility.

When she was 13 years old, Harriet attempted to protect Jim, a fellow slave, from a white overseer. The overseer tried to hit Jim with a two-pound weight as he fled out a door. The weight hit Harriet instead and caused her to have fainting spells the rest of her life. The lump of iron left a deep, scarred dent in her head.

It wasn't long before Harriet decided she could not live as a slave. She wanted to be free. On a dark, starry night, she slipped out. She dodged the human-hunting dogs and the guards who checked travelers at the bridges. She followed the North Star across fields, swamps, and wooded areas. She eventually arrived at Ezekiel Hunn's farm, an Underground Railroad station in Camden, Delaware, where friendly Quakers sheltered her. She had to keep out of sight, for slave-catchers were everywhere. They made money capturing escaped slaves and returning them to their masters.

Harriet worked as a laundress, scrubwoman, cook, and seamstress in Philadelphia. She changed jobs rather frequently during the first year, just to enjoy her newfound freedom. But Harriet could not help thinking about her family. She decided to return to Maryland to rescue her sister and her children. She guided them up the Chesapeake Bay at night in a tiny boat. In a few months, Harriet returned again for more slaves. It was dangerous work, but she was very clever. Altogether, Harriet made 19 trips south, and she helped free over 300 slaves.

Harriet often distracted people who were hunting for her. On one occasion, she carried two live chickens. When she was approached by a man who could have identified her, she dropped the chickens and pretended to chase them. There was so much commotion that no one got a good look at her. Slave owners offered a reward of $40,000 for her capture, dead or alive.

During the Civil War, Harriet served as a spy for three years. She was never caught. After the war, when the slaves were freed, Harriet continued to help others. She took care of black orphans and elderly people. She even started schools for blacks in the South. She was terribly poor, yet she helped hundreds of people during her life. She died on March 10, 1913, at the age of 93.

In the blank beside each statement, write *fact, assumption,* or *value statement.*

_____   1. Harriet Tubman was very poor.

_____   2. Slaves should be free.

_____   3. There was a reward for Tubman's capture.

_____   4. If Harriet were alive today, she would be
                                      pleased with the progress in civil rights.

_____   5. It is worth making personal sacrifices to
                                      help others.

_____   6. If Harriet had had an adequate amount of
                                      money, she would have helped twice as
                                      many slaves to freedom.

_____   7. Harriet served as a spy during the Civil War.

8. Which of the following values are clearly reflected in Harriet Tubman's life activities?
   Put a check mark beside the statements that are supported by facts in the story.

   _____   a. People ought to have personal freedom.

   _____   b. Education should be available to those who wish to learn.

   _____   c. Spying is a justifiable way of helping people gain their freedom.

   _____   d. If people aren't willing to help themselves, they don't deserve our help.

   _____   e. Personal danger should not keep you from helping others.

   _____   f. All living things deserve to be protected.

9. The reading notes that Harriet was a remarkable woman. Which one of her
   accomplishments listed below do you think made her most remarkable?
   Put a check mark beside the statement.

   _____   a. Harriet figured out how she could escape to the North.

   _____   b. Harriet learned to deal with her fainting spells.

   _____   c. Harriet risked her life to help others.

   _____   d. Harriet set up schools for blacks after the war.

   _____   e. Harriet took care of black orphans and elderly people.

10. Explain your reasoning for your choice for number 9.

_____

_____

_____

Busy Builders

Except for human beings, the beaver is the most influential living agent of change. Beavers build dams of branches and logs, which they use as homes. In the process, they cut down huge numbers of trees and form new lakes and ponds. These bodies of water then serve as new habitats for millions of additional aquatic plants and animals.

As cities and suburbs expand, they cut into the natural waterways, fields, and forests where beavers live. Beth Sweetland, a researcher with People for the Ethical Treatment of Animals, deplores the fact that developers simply kill the beavers without thinking about how the loss of these active creatures will affect the ecosystem. Sweetland would like to see builders and state officials transport these clever rodents to areas where they could live undisturbed.

Beavers were once near extinction in the Midwest because of fur trapping, but they are now plentiful. Growth in the beaver population may be linked to the decline in the value of pelts. Top price for a beaver pelt is now $20 to $28, compared with $80 to $100 only a few years ago.

Lame Stowell, a Wisconsin wildlife damage control specialist, points out that even when beaver damage is not widespread throughout a state, the impact on an individual landowner can be disastrous. If the owner of a fruit orchard near a stream has half his or her trees destroyed, it can mean financial ruin. Likewise, lake property owners who have had their homes flooded for weeks when the outlets from their lakes have been plugged by beaver dams can suffer enormous financial losses. To deal with these problems, Wisconsin officials provided a bounty for beaver hides, resulting in the elimination of about 11,000 beavers of an estimated population of 140,000. The state of Minnesota spent $3 per beaver to kill 100,000 of the several hundred thousand beavers roaming the lakes and streams of that midwestern state in the 1990s.

Animal activists recognize that valuable trees must be protected, but they feel that the indiscriminate slaughter of beavers is not the answer. In Illinois, they have urged officials to inform property owners that they can protect valuable trees by covering the lower trunks with wire mesh. Beavers have difficulty gnawing through the mesh.

It is obvious that people throughout the Midwest recognize that beaver populations are a problem. However, they often disagree regarding the best ways to deal with the problem because they hold very different values.

1. Which of the following value positions would a *champion of animals* (an animal activist) probably support? Put a check mark beside the ones you select.

   _____   a. People should be paid handsomely for beaver pelts.

   _____   b. People should have a greater right to land than animals have.

   _____   c. Animals should be treated humanely (kindly).

   _____   d. All the parts of our environment should work together harmoniously.

   _____   e. We must be careful when we tinker with or change parts of the ecosystem.

   _____   f. People should have a right to protect their valuable trees.

   _____   g. Killing beavers is all right if there are plenty of them.

2. Which of the statements that you checked above do you think the animal activists would feel most strongly about?

   _____

   _____

   _____

   _____

   _____

   Why?

   _____

   _____

   _____

   _____

   _____

   _____

3. Which of the following value positions would a *wildlife damage control officer* likely support? Put a check mark beside them.

_____ a. If we are being overrun by rodents, we must take steps to get rid of them.

_____ b. We should recognize that nature has a way of balancing out populations of animals.

_____ c. The protection of valuable property must be seen as a major priority.

_____ d. Landowners have a right to protection.

_____ e. Hunting and trapping should be recognized as legitimate human activities.

_____ f. The formation of new lakes and ponds by beavers is so important that these animals should be protected.

_____ g. States do not have a right to deal with problems that only affect individual property owners.

4. Which of the statements that you checked in question 3 do you think the damage control officer would feel most strongly about?

_____

_____

_____

_____

_____

Why?

_____

_____

_____

_____

_____

_____

III.

Who, What, Where, When, Why, and How:

Understanding How Conditions or Events in a Story or Report Relate to Each Other

Introduction

We all recognize that stories, historical accounts, and reports of current events provide us with organized bodies of facts, opinions, and impressions. Stories normally have characters, settings, and plots, and they may have themes or unstated messages as well. Historical accounts by their nature typically highlight a series of past occurrences. Reports of current events, on the other hand, usually focus on social developments, scientific achievements, or happenings in the worlds of the arts, literature, or nature.

As we attempt to make sense of these narratives and recorded observations, we must figure out how the conditions or events are organized and how they relate to one another. In the readings that follow, five kinds of relationships can be seen:

1. *How some of the conditions or events described influence other conditions or events in the story.* For example, very dry weather may prompt farmers to dig irrigation ditches in order to save their crops.

2. *How a solution to a problem is developed.* In fighting a disease, for example, medical researchers may have to test several types of medicine before they find a cure.

3. *How events and the explanations given for these events relate to each other.* For example, imagine that a judge must decide who most deserves the treasure recovered from a sunken ship: the descendents of the ship's original owners, or the people who discover and recover the treasure. Each group has a reason for its claim.

4. *Changes in the main character's point of view regarding himself or herself and specific conditions described in the narrative.* For example, a small child's attitude toward dogs may change after the child is bitten.

5. *How conditions affect the techniques people use in solving problems.* For example, detectives and criminal investigators, who were not present at the time a crime was committed, often have to collect small fragments of evidence to convict a criminal.

All the questions require you to read carefully and provide you with some practical ways to analyze what you have read.

The Black Death

You may have heard of the old nursery rhyme, "Ring-a-ring-o'roses." The four short lines simply state:

> Ring-a-ring o'roses,
> A pocketful of posies,
> A-tisho, a-tisho,
> We all fall down!

You may be more familiar with a more popular version:

> Ring-around-the-roses,
> A pocket full of posies,
> Ashes, ashes,
> We all fall down!

This innocent sounding verse sprang up in the streets of London in 1665 when the Black Death struck England. The "ring o'roses" referred to the ringed, red spots or blisters that appeared on victims of the disease. The "pocket full of posies" was a reference to the flowers that fearful individuals often stuffed in their clothing to ward off evil spirits or to get rid of the smell of death and sickness. "A-tisho" relates to sneezing, which was an early symptom of the disease.

"Ashes, ashes," supposedly refers to the burning of a dead person's clothing and personal belongings to help stop the spread of the plague. The problem with this version is that it should *follow* falling down dead.

"We all fall down" simply explained what happened next. An estimated 25 million people all over Europe fell down dead of the plague. Even today, we often say "God bless you" when someone sneezes. It is a wish that they will be protected from the plague.

The citizens of London did not know how to fight the plague, of course. They burned cats, dogs, mice, and rats, but their efforts were too little, too late. By 1666, more than 68,000 Londoners had died. On September 2, 1666, a fire broke out in the heart of London. The fire burned for four days and left four fifths of the city in ruins. Londoners lost their public buildings, homes, and businesses, but the fire also wiped out the unsanitary conditions which had helped to spread the plague.

Civilizations have suffered from outbreaks of the plague since very early times. Unfortunately, the disease is easily transmitted from one person to another, and it brings death to a very high proportion of its victims. Sometimes up to 90 percent of a population becomes infected.

Fleas carry this tragic sickness, and rodents normally spread it. Fur trappers brought the last major outbreak of the plague to Europe in 1910 from eastern Siberia. Marmot furs had become very popular in Europe, and both the Mongols and the Chinese hunted the little squirrellike creatures almost to extinction. The traders shipped their furs slowly across the 4,000-mile Trans-Siberian Railroad, and the customers who bought the furs got a little something extra: fleas and bubonic plague.

Modern antibiotics can cure most people who contract the plague today if treatment is started within a few hours. If treatment is delayed more than a day, however, 50 percent of the victims will die.

I. This report explains how the people of London reacted to the Black Death. Answer the following questions based on the report.

1. Although the Londoners did not understand why people died from the plague, they tried to fight the disease in several ways. List two things they did to combat the Black Plague.

   _____

   _____

   _____

   _____

   _____

2. How did the fire of 1666 affect the plague?

   _____

   _____

   _____

   _____

   _____

3. What is there about the plague that makes it particularly threatening to large populations of people?

   _____

   _____

   _____

   _____

   _____

II. This report clearly indicates that the plague has not disappeared from the earth. Answer the following questions about how this disease affects life today.

1. Describe two steps that could be taken to safeguard people from the plague today.

_____

_____

_____

_____

_____

2. Why do you think we still say "God bless you" today when someone sneezes, even though we don't see any evidences of the plague around us?

_____

_____

_____

_____

_____

The Spy Who Came in From the Sea

It was a cold, starless night in the spring of 1943 when the dark silhouette of a submarine glided silently through the Strait of Gibraltar and sank quietly beneath the waves in the Mediterranean Sea. The submarine was carrying an extraordinary gift for the German high command. The gift was part of the continuing game of cat and mouse being played by spies and intelligence officers attached to all armies during World War II. The Germans and the Italians were fighting against the British and Americans in Europe. Each of the opposing sides tried to mislead the other about their military plans.

By the spring of 1943, the tide of the battle was beginning to turn against Germany. A German Army that had once numbered 285,000 troops had been destroyed at Stalingrad in Russia, and the Germans had surrendered to the Allies (British and American troops) in North Africa. In order to defeat the Germans, the Allies now had to get from North Africa to Sicily without letting the Germans know where their landing would take place. If the Germans had that information, they could easily sink the ships before the troops could come ashore. The Allies hoped to convince the Germans that their armies would be landing at a very different location—perhaps southern France or Greece instead of Sicily.

Lieutenant Ewen Montague devised a plan to fool the Germans. He suggested using the body of a dead soldier. The body, carrying false documents about a fake landing plan, was to be dropped near Spain to throw the Germans off the track. Spain was chosen because it was pro-German, even though it was not in the war. The British knew the Spanish authorities would be sure to turn any Allied secrets over to the Germans.

The body of a pneumonia victim was found. It was dressed to look like a British officer. The body, plus a sealed briefcase carrying the fake documents, was dropped overboard from the submarine, and it washed ashore at the Spanish town of Huelva. In a few weeks, the Spanish authorities informed the British Army that they had recovered the body and buried it. There was no comment about the briefcase that floated ashore with the body.

The British immediately inquired about the briefcase. A large number of messages were sent back and forth between the British and the Spanish authorities. A week later, the briefcase was handed over. When the British saw that the briefcase had been opened and sealed up again, they knew that the Germans had read the misleading information. The Germans lessened their defenses in the very areas on Sicily where General Patton and his troops came ashore. The false documents describing the fake landing plans eventually saved thousands of lives.

When intelligence officers and spies serve their countries during times of war, they have to be very clever. Answer the following questions about deception and strategy.

1. Why did the British want to appear to be eager to get back the briefcase that floated ashore with the dead soldier?

    _____

    _____

    _____

2. Why were the dead soldier and the briefcase dropped off near Spain?

    _____

    _____

    _____

3. What could you look for to see if the enemy has received false information given by you and accepted it as true?

    _____

    _____

    _____

    _____

4. What is the assumption behind the use of undercover agents and spies?

    _____

    _____

    _____

5. Do you think it would be wise to transmit the same false information to the enemy through more than one avenue of communication? _____ Yes _____ No

    Explain the reason for your answer below.

    _____

    _____

    _____

Gifts From Outer Space

The scientific work used to prepare vehicles for use in outer space has contributed to our everyday lives. Satellites bring us images, information, and even rock concerts from other continents. These "eyes in the skies" watch how crops in Africa are growing to let us know if there is going to be a famine. Satellites provide telephone links and weather forecasts around the globe.

A number of improvements in our lives have evolved from space travel. A running shoe with a new type of cushioned sole comes from developments in clothing and other needs for space explorers. The breathing equipment for firefighters was developed from lightweight materials used in rocket motors.

The National Aeronautics and Space Administration's (NASA) need to know exactly what was happening to all parts of a spacecraft led to a diagnostic tool for cars. A system called Autosense checks working parts in a car against a carefully prepared factory list. It tells what's wrong and suggests what to do about it.

It is necessary in a space mission to know how astronauts' bodies are reacting to weightlessness and oxygen supplies. Sensors on the skin record these reactions. Here on Earth, these same sensors allow doctors to provide similar information to patients with neurological and muscular problems.

One of the most intriguing uses of space research is the rechargeable pacemaker for heart patients. Although astronauts do not wear pacemakers, the batteries they take with them can be recharged for extended use. The system has become so refined that physicians can monitor the heart and reprogram the pacemaker if necessary—without surgery.

Scientific developments in outer space have influenced life on Earth in at least three ways. Answer the following questions in complete sentences.

1. Sometimes we use space instruments for specific purposes on Earth without changing or adapting them very much. Name one of these instruments and explain how we use it.

   _____

   _____

   _____

   _____

   _____

2. Sometimes we use the instruments in much the same way they are used with astronauts or spacecraft but for somewhat different purposes. What are some examples of this kind of use?

_____

_____

_____

_____

_____

3. Sometimes scientists use materials developed for space travel in quite a different way on Earth. What are some examples of this type of use?

_____

_____

_____

_____

_____

Capping the Devil's Cigarette Lighter

On November 3, 1961, an oil well at Gassi Touil in Algeria blew out with such force that it destroyed safety devices. It also sent a 13-inch-thick column of natural gas into the air. Almost immediately a call went out to Houston: "Get Red Adair, and get him quick."

Adair was on his way to Mexico, so he sent his helpers, Boots Hansen and Coots Mathews, to Algeria. The two men fought for a week to control the gushing gas. A sandstorm blew in, filling the air with charged electricity. Some machinery caught fire and the flames spread to the derrick over the oil well. This was followed by a blinding flash and a thunderous bang as the gas exploded.

Red rushed to Gassi Touil. The first things he ordered were water, bulldozers, pipes, and nitroglycerin. Then he ordered a long pole with a hook to pull the damaged pieces of the derrick away from the burning well. While this operation was being carried out, the workers were sprayed constantly with water.

Adair planned the exact spot to plant explosives to cut off oxygen and extinguish the fire. He also planned where to put the hoses to drive away the fire so it would not set off the explosives too soon.

The explosives were shaped into breadlike loaves. One morning before dawn, the crew directing the hoses began spraying the area. They cooled it for six hours while the explosives were prepared. Then the bulldozer with the long pole was backed into place. Adair placed the explosives by hand and quickly rushed out to give the signal to set them off. The bulldozer jumped a foot when the explosion resounded. The Devil's Cigarette Lighter, as the enormous fire was called, was out!

This story makes it clear that extinguishing a fire at a large oil well requires very special techniques. Dangerous conditions make it necessary to work very carefully. Answer the following questions in complete sentences.

1. Red Adair did not go to Gassi Touil when he was first asked. He sent his assistants, Hansen and Mathews. What change in conditions caused him to go to Gassi Touil later?

   _____

   _____

   _____

   _____

2. We put out many fires with water or chemicals. This was not possible with the Gassi Touil fire. What did Red Adair use, and how did it put out the fire?

_____

_____

_____

_____

_____

_____

3. We don't normally use water hoses in an area before we plant explosives. Why did Red Adair do this?

_____

_____

_____

_____

_____

_____

4. The derrick above the well had been damaged by the explosion. Why did Red Adair use a bulldozer with a pole on it to pull the damaged parts away before he placed the explosives?

_____

_____

_____

_____

_____

Fearless Travels into the Unknown

Have you ever been lost in a strange city where no one knew you? Did you think about going to the city hall, a church, or a police station for help? Today we can often get assistance when we are lost. Early travelers, however, were strictly on their own. There were no organizations like the Red Cross to rescue them when they were lost or faced life-threatening situations.

In 1271, 17-year-old Marco Polo and his father and uncle made one of the most daring and dangerous trips in history. They sailed from Italy to Palestine at the eastern end of the Mediterranean Sea and formed a small caravan for their trip across Asia. During their three-year, 4,000-mile journey, they faced frozen mountain ranges, wild animals, bandits, scorching deserts, and blinding sandstorms. The trip was so exhausting that Marco became desperately ill, and the expedition had to be delayed a year while he regained his health.

When Marco, his father, and his uncle finally reached China, the extreme hardships of the journey all seemed worthwhile. They saw landscaped highways, public parks, marinas, and canals with high arched bridges. The marble palaces of the Mongol emperor, Kublai Khan, were unbelievably beautiful. Fortunately for Marco, the emperor cherished and trusted the young man. He gave him the run of the palaces and summer resorts and took him hunting on royal elephants. The gilded carvings in the palace, the artistic decorations, and the spectacular imperial treasures dazzled Marco. The emperor appointed Marco to be his personal emissary and sent him on missions throughout the empire. Marco Polo visited other countries—Indochina, Burma, and Tibet.

Marco marveled at the many fascinating things he observed during his stay in China. He saw "veins of black stones" (coal) and "liquid from the ground" (oil) that burned, and he saw cloth that would not burn (asbestos). He described crocodiles as "huge serpents, 10 paces in length, that could swallow a man whole." Marco was the first Western man to describe China and its bordering countries, the first to outline a route across the Asian continent, and the first European to see the Pacific Ocean. His trip to China lasted 24 years.

When Marco, his father, and his uncle returned to Venice, Italy, in 1295, hardly any of their relatives recognized them. Their servants wouldn't even let them enter their own homes. Marco and his father decided to give a great banquet because many of their friends wondered if they had really gone to China. During the feast, the hosts kept changing their clothes. Then dramatically, they cut the seams in all the garments and let a shower of precious gems fall onto the banquet table. Kublai Khan had given them gifts, but the Polos had exchanged them in Peking for rubies and emeralds, which they could carry more easily.

The world might never have heard about Marco Polo if a war hadn't broken out. Three years after his return, Venice and Genoa declared war on each other. Marco was commanding a galley (warship) when he was taken prisoner. He was thrown in jail. With so much time on his hands, he decided to dictate his descriptions of China to a fellow prisoner. He explained that the Chinese used paper money, how they made silk, and that they observed unusual religious customs.

Marco's book became very popular, and it was translated into many languages. His book inspired later explorers, including Christopher Columbus. Many readers did not believe all the stories in the book, but historians found that Marco had a keen eye and a good memory. Even on his deathbed in 1324, a priest urged him to retract some of his tallest tales. With his last breath Marco declared, "I have not told half of what I saw."

I. Answer the following questions about Marco Polo's spectacular trip.

1. The report states that it was a daring and dangerous trip. What evidence in the report supports this claim?

_____

_____

_____

_____

2. The report focuses more on Marco than on his father and uncle. What made Marco more famous?

_____

_____

_____

_____

3. The Polos visited a culture that was very different from their own. How does this affect the story?

_____

_____

_____

_____

4. The report states that Kublai Khan cherished and trusted Marco. What evidence is there in the report that this was true?

_____

_____

_____

5. The Polos displayed fantastic jewels when their friends questioned the truthfulness of their stories. Do you think this is the best way to convince friends? Explain.

_____

_____

_____

II. Answer the following questions about Marco Polo's influence on others.

1. What evidence is there in the reading that Marco wanted others to make the same trip?

_____

_____

_____

2. The report states that Marco Polo's book inspired other explorers, such as Christopher Columbus. How could this be true, since Marco walked across Asia, and Columbus sailed across the Atlantic Ocean in a ship?

_____

_____

_____

3. Do you think Marco Polo would have been as famous if he hadn't written a book? Explain.

_____

_____

_____

Counting Animal Populations

Scientists often count the number of animals of a certain kind. This helps us know which animals are endangered (dying out). Sometimes it is valuable to know how many fish or land animals are left that can be used for future food supplies.

The best way to count large animals that can be seen out in the open is to use a helicopter. To be more certain the counts are accurate, photographs are also taken. Pictures allow scientists to check their counts later.

Lizards are counted by the "capture, recapture" method. A certain number—60, for example—are caught and marked with paint. Then they are released. Later, in the same area, 60 lizards are caught again. Those with paint are again counted. Let's say there are 10, for example. That gives a 10-to-60 ratio, or six times as many lizards in that area (6 x 60 = 360).

Birds cannot be captured easily, so several people walk through an area of fields, woods, or wetlands where the birds live. They keep the person on either side of them in view. Each person counts all the birds he or she finds within five feet on either side. Then, when all are finished, the results are averaged.

Tiny animals in the ocean must be counted by whipping up a given amount of water, so the solids as well as the water are collected. Samples are placed under a microscope and counted. Scientists know how much water there is in the world. They multiply the number of specimens in the area they counted by the fraction that amount is of the total.

It is obvious from the information given in this account that animals must be counted in different ways. They are counted by sight, capture, or "capture, recapture." Answer the following questions in complete sentences.

1. Name two kinds of animals in the story that are counted by sight.

   _____

   _____

   _____

   _____

   _____

2. Counting animal populations requires time and effort. What is the reasoning behind this great effort?

_____

_____

_____

_____

_____

3. What is the reasoning behind the scientists' use of mathematical ratios in counting animal populations?

_____

_____

_____

_____

_____

_____

4. What is the basic assumption behind the technique of multiplying to find the total number of animals for the world?

_____

_____

_____

_____

_____

The Chisholm Trail

The Chisholm Trail changed the eating habits of America. From 1867 to about 1890, 10 million cattle were driven along this trail. The trail was named for Jesse Chisholm, who never drove cattle. Chisholm was a Scottish-Cherokee trader in the area. The 1,000-mile path that bears his name began in the Rio Grande Valley of Texas and ended at the Union Pacific Depot in Abilene, Kansas.

The trail came into being after the Civil War (which ended in 1865), when much of the South was in ruins. In Texas, there was an accumulation of mixed-breed cattle from Mexico and other places. These cattle were used to feed a meat-hungry war population, most of it in the six New England states.

At a time when eastern shorthorn cattle cost $30 to $40 a head, the longhorns from Texas sold for $3 a head in Abilene. Cattle traders and shippers like Joseph McCoy contracted with ranchers in Abilene to send cattle to him along the Chishom Trail. He would then distribute the animals via railroad.

About 40,000 cattle came up the trail the first year. The cattle were divided into herds of 300 to 3,000 with one drover (cattle driver) for each 250 animals. A chuck wagon, cook, and a herd of mustangs— small, tough, half-wild horses—were part of each drive. In 1876, the King Ranch in southern Texas sent 30,000 head of cattle divided into 12 herds.

Hardships on the trail for cowboys included prairie-dog holes that could break a pony's leg, snakes, Apache and Comanche, rustlers, stampedes, and fierce weather. Theirs was probably the toughest, riskiest job the country has ever known.

A number of factors and conditions influence each other in this story about the Chisholm Trail. Answer the following questions in complete sentences.

1. How did the difference between the cost of cattle in the East and in Texas affect the movement of cattle?

_____

_____

_____

_____

_____

2. The story begins by stating that the Chisholm Trail changed the eating habits of America. How could a trail change eating habits?

_____

_____

_____

_____

_____

3. We don't have arguments today regarding where highways are actually located. What conditions at that time probably caused people to argue about the location of the trail?

_____

_____

_____

_____

_____

4. Barbed wire was invented about the time the Chisholm Trail was being used. How would this invention help the farmers who were growing crops near the trail?

_____

_____

_____

_____

Europe's Mystery People

The Basques remain an enigma (a puzzle) despite centuries of study. They refer to themselves as Euskaldunak or "Speakers of the Euskera." Linguists have failed to link the Basque language with any other tongue, but they do agree that it is difficult to learn. It has been said that the devil himself could not master it after seven years of study.

The Basque homeland is relatively small. It comprises three French regions and four Spanish provinces on the French-Spanish border, where the Pyrenees Mountains meet the Cantabrian coast. This location has made the Basques vulnerable, and they have been repeatedly invaded by Iberians, Romans, Franks, Moors, Normans, and others. The Basques would like to be free from French and Spanish rule, but so far their violent struggles have not brought freedom.

Basques were Europe's first whalers and may have visited the New World before 1492. They made up the largest part of Columbus's crews. During the 16th century, Basque vessels carried 80 percent of the shipping to the Americas.

During the 1830s, Basque immigrants began settling interior regions of Uruguay and Argentina as sheepherders. With the discovery of gold in North America, many Basques moved there. By the 1860s, when the gold ran out, Basques were becoming the American West's leading sheepherders. The broad, sparsely populated plains were ideal for raising animals. The Basques' success was attributed to a practice called *transhumance,* meaning the seasonal movement of livestock in search of different pastures.

Today large colonies of Basques live in California, Nevada, and Idaho, while smaller groups live in Washington, Oregon, Arizona, New Mexico, Texas, Colorado, Wyoming, and Montana. Since the early 1970s, interest in the Basques has grown, and a center for Basque studies has been established at the University of Nevada in Reno.

This story demonstrates that the Basques were influenced by a variety of factors and conditions. Answer the following questions about the Basques in complete sentences.

1. How did the location of the Basques' homeland in the Pyrenees Mountains affect their early history?

_____

_____

_____

2. The Basques were close to the sea, and they had pasturelands. How did these two geographic factors influence their lives?

_____

_____

_____

_____

_____

_____

3. How did the practice of transhumance affect the lives of the Basques?

_____

_____

_____

_____

_____

4. What factor led to a center for Basque studies at the University of Nevada?

_____

_____

_____

_____

IV.

Why the Chicken Crossed the Road:

Recognizing Cause-Effect Relationships

Introduction

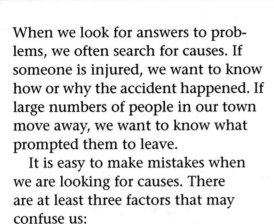

When we look for answers to problems, we often search for causes. If someone is injured, we want to know how or why the accident happened. If large numbers of people in our town move away, we want to know what prompted them to leave.

It is easy to make mistakes when we are looking for causes. There are at least three factors that may confuse us:

1. No Cause-Effect Relationship

When two events happen one after another, we cannot assume that the first *caused* the second to happen. A boat may whistle just before it docks, but the whistle doesn't cause the ship to dock. A dog may walk around in circles before it lies down, but walking in circles doesn't cause the dog to lie down.

2. Necessary Preconditions

Sometimes certain conditions must be established before an event can occur. These are called *necessary preconditions*. They are not causes. We may agree that we will play soccer on Friday if it is clear. However, clear weather doesn't *cause* us to play soccer; it simply *makes it possible* for us to play. Likewise, we may say that we can't buy a bike unless we have money. Having money, however, doesn't cause us to buy a bike.

3. Single Causes and Multiple Causes

Some effects are brought about by a *single cause*, while others result from *multiple causes*. Lightning may strike your television set and put it out of commission. Only one factor—lightning—is responsible for the destruction of the set. On the other hand, an automobile accident may be caused by a number of factors, such as poor visibility, slippery pavements, slow reaction time on the part of the driver, and excessive speed. Under such circumstances, it is difficult to know how much each factor contributed to the crash.

Multiple causes may occur all at once, as in the case of the automobile accident just described, or they may occur as a series of events. Let's say you hear someone scream in a nearby room. While running to help, you fall over a toy and tear your clothing. In this case, a series of factors caused you to tear your clothing.

I. See if you can choose the four cause-effect statements in the sentences below. Put a check mark beside your choices.

_____ a. The sun shone, and the birds sang as the baby was born.

_____ b. As the dog came in through the open door, the water boiled over.

_____ c. Many of the eagles were dying because of the water pollution.

_____ d. Her asthma is made worse by the cosmetics she uses.

_____ e. As the church bell rang, the firefighters made their first run.

_____ f. The melons had been picked too early, so they weren't fit to eat.

_____ g. The gully deepened as rainwater gushed down the hill.

_____ h. Lightning struck as the bus entered the park.

II. *Necessary preconditions* don't actually make things happen, but they are required in order to allow an event to take place. Select the five statements below that describe necessary preconditions. Put a check mark beside your choices.

_____ a. The gravel thrown up by passing cars destroyed the flowers.

_____ b. Time heals hurt feelings.

_____ c. Mandy had to get permission from her mother before she could go out.

_____ d. To become a U.S. senator, a person must be elected or appointed.

_____ e. The riots were started by starving peasants.

_____ f. You must register for classes before you can attend them.

_____ g. If you allow more time, the opposing sides can work out a solution.

_____ h. We must wait for the mud to dry before we can enter the field.

III. Many events have *multiple causes.* In other words, several factors bring about the results. Which five of the following statements describe multiple causes? Put a check mark beside your choices.

_____ a. Randy was very unhappy in his job because of the long hours, the low pay, and the poor working conditions.

_____ b. Tom was very frightened, tired, and confused, and he was unable to help the strangers.

_____ c. The searchers were unable to find the necklace because it was dark in color and the light was very dim.

_____ d. The calendar fell to the floor.

_____ e. The band soon stopped playing.

_____ f. The scorching sun and hot winds dried up the flowers.

_____ g. The dog stopped barking, and the cat quieted down.

_____ h. Time and loving care helped him recover from his illness.

In the following exercises, you will be asked to determine the types of causal relationships described in a series of readings.

Magicians and Escape Artists

David Copperfield, often dubbed one of the greatest modern magicians, has performed many amazing feats during his career. He has performed the world-famous "disappearing Statue of Liberty" stunt and has broken out of a chained, locked safe seconds before the building it was sitting in was scheduled to be demolished by dynamite. These feats were performed in front of a live audience and televised across the world.

During a recent, wonderfully entertaining show, Copperfield also performed many stunts. Some memorable examples included dancing handkerchiefs, Copperfield sawing himself in half, and Copperfield causing his assistant to disappear.

The finale was the best part of the performance, though! Copperfield stood astride his black motorcycle and was lifted into the air. From atop the platform, with a burst of smoke, he vanished. Seconds later, to the excitement of the crowd, he reappeared in the middle of the audience, apparently still on the motorcycle. Everyone realizes that there is some sort of "trick" or "catch" to these performances, but they are thrilling nonetheless.

Harry Houdini, one of the best magicians of all time, executed some of the most extraordinary stunts the world has ever seen. He advertised one of these stunts as "My Challenge to Death." He claimed that he could escape from a packing case underwater. Crowds gathered, fascinated.

Carpenters constructed the heavy container. Houdini stepped inside, his hands handcuffed, while the workers finished hammering in nails. A thick rope was tied securely around the case. A crane onboard a tugboat lifted the packing case and lowered it into the water, where it disappeared from sight. A tense few minutes followed.

Suddenly the packing case was hoisted out of the water with Houdini, safe and sound, sitting on top of it, enjoying the cheers and applause. The case was brought to the pier so the spectators could see that it was still sealed tightly.

How did Houdini manage it? For starters, the handcuffs were fake. They were easily opened by a secret spring. Also he took with him, hidden, a pair of nail cutters.

As soon as he got underwater, he cut enough nails to push away a section of the lid. He stepped out and sat on the boards, pushing them back into place. For a few moments on the way back to the pier, the box was out of sight. That gave the carpenters a chance to pick out any broken nails and put in new ones.

However one looks at it, it was a daring feat. Many things could go wrong, so Houdini had to be very calm and extremely careful. Perhaps these qualities are the real secret of all great magicians.

Complete the following exercise as directed.

1. Circle the *necessary preconditions* for Harry Houdini to perform his "death challenge."

    a. The box had to be prepared for the stunt.

    b. Houdini needed a pair of nail cutters.

    c. Houdini needed a standard pair of handcuffs.

2. Match the following causes with their resulting effects. Write the letter of the effect on the right next to its cause on the left.

    _____ Copperfield carried out a trick with a member of his act.

    _____ Houdini advertised his stunt.

    _____ Houdini was safe from harm.

    a. The crowd cheered and applauded.

    b. Crowds gathered to watch.

    c. His assistant disappeared.

What are the causal relationships in the following statements? Circle the letter of your answer.

3. As soon as Houdini got underwater, he cut enough nails to push away a section of the lid. This allowed him to escape.

    a. single cause

    b. multiple causes

    c. necessary precondition

    d. no cause-effect

4. Houdini stepped aside while the workers finished hammering in nails.

    a. single cause

    b. multiple causes

    c. necessary precondition

    d. no cause-effect

5. When Houdini touched the secret spring, the handcuffs opened.

   a. single cause

   b. multiple causes

   c. necessary precondition

   d. no cause-effect

6. The carpenters were given time to pick out any broken nails and put in new ones.

   a. single cause

   b. multiple causes

   c. necessary precondition

   d. no cause-effect

7. Why did you choose the answer you selected in question 6?

   _____

   _____

   _____

   _____

8. Which of the following statements involve *multiple causes*? Circle the letter(s) of your answer(s).

   a. Houdini performed, people watched, and he became famous.

   b. The case was brought to the pier. Houdini was sitting on top of it.

   c. David Copperfield reappeared, people were amazed, and they clapped wildly.

9. Why did you choose the answer(s) you selected in question 8?

_____

_____

_____

_____

_____

Identify the causal relationships of the sentences below. Write *single cause, multiple causes, necessary precondition, no cause-effect* on the lines provided.

10. A crane lowered the packing case. The crane was located on a tug.

_____

11. Houdini advertised his stunt, people told each other, and huge crowds gathered.

_____

12. Houdini was lowered into the water. This cut off his supply of air and light.

_____

13. Why did you choose the answer you selected in question 12?

_____

_____

_____

_____

_____

An Unbelievable Ride to Victory

Shortly before midnight, Dick King and his Zulu servant boy crept silently to the edge of the water at the far end of South Africa's Durban Harbor. It was a dark night, but they could detect the outlines of the small boat and horses waiting for them. They crawled into the boat and rowed quickly toward Salisbury Island, trailing their horses behind them.

Dick King and his small companion knew that the lives of hundreds of British soldiers and citizens depended on their death-defying journey that night. The Boer (Dutch) farmers had surrounded the small British territory. The British were fighting bravely, but they were outnumbered six to one. The British were running out of supplies, and they were exhausted. Without reinforcements, they would succumb in less than six weeks.

The Dutch farmers were so confident of a victory that they had already announced their new nation to the world. They named it the Republic of Natal. The situation was desperate for the British. There were no reinforcements within 300 miles of Durban, and communications at the time were very slow and cumbersome. There were no telephones or radios.

Dick King realized that he had to get to Grahamstown, a British military base far to the south. He knew that only a young man with hunting skills and a knowledge of the rugged backcountry would have half a chance of getting through. He and his servant boy, Ndongeni, saddled the horses on Salisbury Island and waited for the tide to go out. As the sea swept out, a wide stretch of beach was exposed. The two riders galloped down the sandy shore, outflanking the nearby Boer patrols.

Dick King and Ndongeni rode during the night and slept during the day. Even though there were night-feeding crocodiles in the rivers, they often had to dismount and swim across streams, leading their horses behind them. When they finally reached the veldt (grass-covered plains), there were new dangers. Lions and warrior tribes lived in those regions.

After 200 miles of exhausting riding through treacherous terrain, Ndongeni had to give up. King himself became so weak and sick that he, too, had to rest two days to recover his strength. He struggled on alone, desperately hoping that another rider might come along to replace him and complete the journey. His horse also reached the limits of its endurance. At Butterworth, a friendly trader exchanged a fresh mount for King's weary pony, and King continued on, dazed and disheartened.

On June 4, 11 days after he had set out on his epic ride, Dick King rode up the main street of Grahamstown and delivered his message to the commander of the garrison. A month later, he was back in Durban with a contingent of seaborne troops who quickly relieved the beleaguered English settlement. The grateful citizens of Durban erected a monument to Dick King, which stands in the center of the largest city park.

Read each statement below about an event in this narrative. Put a check mark beside the answer that best completes the statement.

1. When Dick King and Ndongeni waited on Salisbury Island for the tide to go out, this was an example of

    _____ a. necessary precondition.

    _____ b. single cause.

    _____ c. multiple causes.

    _____ d. no cause-effect.

2. When a friend provided a boat and two horses for the trip, this was an example of

    _____ a. necessary precondition.

    _____ b. single cause.

    _____ c. multiple causes.

    _____ d. no cause-effect.

3. If the British garrison had surrendered because they were exhausted and out of supplies, this would have been an example of

    _____ a. necessary precondition.

    _____ b. single cause.

    _____ c. multiple causes.

    _____ d. no cause-effect.

4. When the Dutch farmers named their new country the Republic of Natal, this was an example of

    _____ a. necessary precondition.

    _____ b. single cause.

    _____ c. multiple causes.

    _____ d. no cause-effect.

5. When the narrative points out that the situation was desperate for the British, this was an example of

_____ a. necessary precondition.

_____ b. single cause.

_____ c. multiple causes.

_____ d. no cause-effect.

6. When King realized that only a young man with hunting skills and a knowledge of the rugged backcountry could succeed, this was an example of

_____ a. necessary precondition.

_____ b. single cause.

_____ c. multiple causes.

_____ d. no cause-effect.

7. When King and Ndongeni swam the streams and pulled their horses behind them, this was an example of

_____ a. necessary precondition.

_____ b. single cause.

_____ c. multiple causes.

_____ d. no cause-effect.

8. When King became so weak that he had to rest for two days, this was an example of

_____ a. necessary precondition.

_____ b. single cause.

_____ c. multiple causes.

_____ d. no cause-effect.

9. When a friendly trader exchanged a fresh mount for King's weary pony, this was an example of

_____ a. necessary precondition.

_____ b. single cause.

_____ c. multiple causes.

_____ d. no cause-effect.

10. When Dick King rode up the main street of Grahamstown and delivered his message to the commanders of the garrison, this was an example of

_____ a. necessary precondition.

_____ b. single cause.

_____ c. multiple causes.

_____ d. no cause-effect.

Rescue of the USS S-5

The prefix *sub-* means "below," and the aptly named submarine is a ship that travels underwater. The submarine was invented by the British in 1620. Today it is mainly used as a vehicle of war and is usually powered by nuclear energy. The submarine is very important because it makes up a large part of the naval forces in the world today.

Submarines are able to travel on or below the water's surface. To submerge a submarine, special tanks at the front and rear of the ship are flooded. The added water weight in these ballast tanks makes the ship "neutrally buoyant." The submarine can then glide through the water, much like a plane through the air, guided by diving planes. The planes enable the submarine to move up, down, or straight through the water.

A submarine can resurface in two ways. Compressed air can be used to blow water out of the ballast tanks, or the diving planes can be tilted up, angling the submarine to the surface. The procedure sounds simple, but it took many years to perfect the process.

On an August day in 1920, the U.S. Navy's large S-5 submarine left Boston on a training mission to Baltimore. It passed the ship *Alanthus,* which was about to be retired from service.

The S-5 prepared to dive. As soon as the dive began, Commander Charles

Cooke knew something was wrong. He ran for the control room. The air valve had been left open and water was rushing in.

Men climbed torpedoes to reach the valve on the ceiling, but the rush of water hurled them back. The water in the bow dragged the submarine down. It hit bottom and rammed into the seafloor.

Suddenly battery acid was spilling and mixing with water. This formed poisonous chlorine gas. The crew retreated up through the vessel. Commander Cooke thought the stern might be out of the water. He worked his way up.

The tiller room seemed to be above water. Cooke called for a drill and cut a hole through the steel plate. Air could get in, but it took hours to make the hole larger with hand drills. Cooke waved a dirty undershirt through the hole when it was light.

The mate of the *Alanthus* noticed something on the water. The ship had no radio, so they ran a hose and pumps to deliver air to the submarine.

It was sundown before the liner *General Goethals* appeared. This ship *did* have a radio, and it immediately sent out an SOS. In the meantime, men from the *Goethals* brought pry bars to the sub. They worked at the plate and after several hours tore it loose. All the men from the submarine were rescued.

Identify the causal relationships in the sentences below. Write *single cause, multiple causes, necessary precondition,* or *no cause-effect* on the line provided.

1. The air valve was left open; water was rushing in.

   _____

2. The *General Goethals* had a radio. It was able to send an SOS.

   _____

3. Commander Cooke cut a hole with a drill, and air rushed into the submarine.

   _____

4. Water flooded the interior, and as the sub became heavier, it sank toward the seafloor.

   _____

5. Chlorine gas began to build up. The men of the S-5 survived the wreck.

   _____

6. Which of the following choices are *necessary preconditions* for a submarine to begin to submerge? Circle the letter of all correct answers.

   a. It must be afloat.

   b. It must be powered by a nuclear energy source.

   c. The diving planes must be working properly.

   d. The ballast tanks must be empty.

   e. The submarine must be neutrally buoyant.

7. Match the causes with their resulting effects. Write the letter of the effect on the right next to its cause on the left.

   _____ The men used pry bars.

   _____ The *Geothals* arrived in time.

   _____ The ballast tanks were filled.

   a. The submarine was neutrally buoyant.

   b. The plate was torn loose.

   c. No one perished.

8. What is the original cause of the S-5 submarine sinking?

   _____

   What type of causal relationship is this?

   _____

9. "Suddenly battery acid was spilling and mixing with water. This formed poisonous chlorine gas." This is an example of which type of causal relationship? Circle the letter of your choice.

   a. multiple causes

   b. single cause

   c. necessary precondition

   d. no cause-effect

10. Which of the following statements are examples of a multiple cause-effect relationship? Put a check mark beside them.

   _____ a. Cooke waved a dirty undershirt. The mate of the *Alanthus* noticed something in the water. The *Alanthus* crew ran a hose and pumps.

   _____ b. The S-5 sailed past the *Alanthus*. The *Alanthus* delivered air to the submarine.

   _____ c. The water rushed in through the open air valve. The men were hurled back, unable to close the valve, and the submarine rammed into the seafloor.

   _____ d. The men from the *Geothals* brought pry bars. The steel plate was torn loose. The crew was rescued.

11. Which of the following pairs of statements are events that occur together, but that have *no causal relationship*? Put a check mark before your choice(s).

   _____ a. The S-5 submarine leaves on a training mission; the S-5 passes the Liberty ship *Alanthus*.

   _____ b. The *Geothals* arrived; an SOS was sent out.

   _____ c. The plate was torn loose; the crew was safely rescued.

   _____ d. The tiller room was above water; Cooke called for a drill and made a hole.

Making the World Safe for All Living Things

The conservation and preservation of wildlife is very important, because animals that will exist in the future must descend from the animals that are living today. If a species dies out, there is no way we can reintroduce it to the world.

Nature is a delicate balance that must be maintained. The destruction of one species affects many other species. Weasels and chickens are a good example. As long as the weasel has an adequate supply of mice and other foods, it is not likely to attack chickens. If its normal food supply is not sufficient, however, the weasel will seek out chickens.

Because the food chain is so fragile, human beings have tried to create ways to protect and preserve nature's balance. Animal sanctuaries, wildlife parks, and wildlife preserves have all been established. Many countries, such as those in Africa, have set aside wildlife preserves in which hunting is forbidden. Elephants, lions, and tigers in these areas are now safe from hunters.

The wardens who police these preserves do not have an easy job. Two such wardens, Rolf Rohmer and David Taylor, once had a frightening encounter with a strange animal.

It was a routine assignment. Rohmer and Taylor scanned the wild-animal enclosure with field glasses before entering it to move a giraffe. Once inside, all looked peaceful, until one of a pair of "horsey creatures" began to move slowly toward them. Suddenly it broke into a wild trot and was soon close enough to be identified as an onager, a species of wild ass.

"Look at those legs go!" Rohmer exclaimed. "By golly, it's got its ears laid back." Even more frightening, the onager's lips were drawn back, and it began to make an ugly, piglike, squealing noise.

"Jump!" Rohmer yelled.

Both men managed to leap from the ground and climb into the same tree. The onager screeched to a halt, then stood at the base of the tree, biting furiously at the bark. A falling twig irritated the crazed animal further, and it made a standing leap, just grazing Taylor's shoe heel.

Half an hour later, the situation had not changed. The men needed something to break the stalemate. They planned their strategy: They would break off a tree branch and stuff it into the sleeve of Taylor's jacket. Perhaps the makeshift scarecrow would be enough to distract the onager while the men escaped.

The strategy worked! The onager grabbed the stuffed jacket and flung it down. It began to stamp, rip, and gnaw on it with a ferocious zeal, utterly absorbed. The men, hearts in mouths, dropped quietly to the ground. They ran to the fence and got through the gate, barely managing to slam the frame shut before the 500-pound onager hurled itself at the metal.

The men soon learned that the onager had already severely mauled two park workers. After a merciful death, the onager was examined by a veterinarian. It had a tapeworm cyst as large as a table-tennis ball embedded in a frontal lobe of its brain. The onager had been literally driven crazy by what started out as a tiny beetle on a blade of grass.

Circle the letter(s) of the best answer or answers to each question below.

1. Which of the following statements include a *cause-effect* relationship?

   a. Animals living today will be the ancestors of the creatures to come.

   b. Weasels like to eat mice, but they may also eat chickens.

   c. Rohmer and Taylor scanned the enclosure before entering.

   d. We should not allow species to die out.

2. Which of the following statements contain *multiple causes*?

   a. Both men managed to climb into the same tree.

   b. When animal species became endangered, biologists recognized the problem, and animal preserves were established.

   c. The men slammed the gate shut before the 500-pound onager hurled itself against the metal.

3. Which of the following are *necessary preconditions* for the establishment of animal preserves?

   a. Large amounts of land are required.

   b. Money is required to meet costs.

   c. Elephants are required.

   d. Permission from the United Nations is required.

4. Why did you choose the answer(s) you selected in question 3?

   _____

   _____

   _____

   _____

5. Identify the causal relationships of the sentences below. Write *single cause, multiple causes, necessary precondition,* or *no cause-effect* on the lines provided.

   a. Because the food chain is so fragile, people have raised funds and tried to create ways to protect its balance.

   _____

   b. The onager screeched to a halt. It bit furiously at the bark on the tree.

   _____

   c. The men had to divert the onager's attention in order to get away.

   _____

   d. The onager had a tapeworm cyst. Its brain was affected, and it behaved in a crazed manner.

   _____

   e. The onager left its companion; it broke into a wild trot.

   _____

   f. After a merciful death, the onager was examined by a veterinarian.

   _____

   g. The onager ate a blade of grass with a beetle on it. The beetle entered its digestive system, and the onager went crazy.

   _____

   h. The men needed something to break the stalemate. They decided on a strategy, the strategy worked, and they escaped.

   _____

Clever but Deadly

Most people think of spiders as "repulsive insects." Neither of these words accurately describes the more than 29,000 kinds of spiders found throughout the world. Spiders are arachnids, not insects, and they have some amazing abilities.

Spiders differ from insects in that they have eight legs rather than six, and they lack wings and antennae. All spiders have fangs and most can be poisonous, but they generally do not bite people unless they are frightened or injured.

Spiders can live almost anywhere: fields, swamps, caves, woods, or deserts. They are also very helpful. Spiders feed on insects, many of which are harmful to humans. They vary in dimension from the size of a head of a pin to the size of a person's hand. One of the most amazing characteristics of some spiders is the ability to spin silk and construct webs.

Before a spider makes a web, it must have two places for support, such as the surfaces of a corner of a room, two bushes, or other structures that offer anchoring places about three feet from each other. Preferably, the web will be made outside over a grassy place where plenty of insects fly.

When all is ready, including testing the wind, glands in the spider's abdomen produce silk in a liquid form and push it through the spinnerets on the spider's body. When the liquid is exposed to the air, it immediately hardens. The wind helps carry the strand to the opposite support. The first strand is a bridge on which the spider can travel. The spider makes strong threads for the main outline of the web and sticky, fill-in threads to trap prey. The spider does not stick to the web because it has oil on its feet. When it is wet outdoors, the spider's web loses its stickiness.

When the work is finished, the spider waits for something to fly into its web and get stuck. As soon as this happens, the spider weaves strands of silk around its prey. The spider then bites its prey and injects it with venom.

The spider was the inspiration for the poem that begins, "'Come into my parlor,' said the spider to the fly." The fly was to be the spider's dinner. Imagine building a home that doubles as a trap for your food. The spider seems to be content with this arrangement.

Identify the causal relationships of the following sentences. Write *single cause, multiple causes, necessary precondition,* or *no cause-effect* on the lines provided.

1. Liquid silk is exposed to air; liquid silk hardens.

_____

2. Spiders have protective skin; spiders do not have bones.

   _____

3. Spiders have oil on their feet; spiders do not stick to their own webs.

   _____

4. Spiders have fangs; spiders are poisonous.

   _____

5. Insects on which spiders feed live in fields; spiders can live in fields.

   _____

6. Name three *necessary preconditions* for a spider to be classified as an arachnid and not an insect.

   _____

7. Match the following causes with their resulting effects. Write the letter of the effect on the right next to its cause on the left.

   _____ Spiders feed on harmful insects.

   _____ Rain soaks the spider's web.

   _____ The spider stings the insect.

   a. The insect dies.

   b. The insects are not caught in the web.

   c. Spiders help humans.

8. Which of the following statements are *necessary preconditions* for the spider to catch its prey?

   a. The web must be sticky.

   b. The spider must be poisonous.

   c. The spider must have spun a web.

   d. The spider must sting its prey.

9. Complete the following sentence with the appropriate answer from the story: Two places for support located about three feet apart are a necessary precondition for

   _____.

The Red Army

There are 4,500 different types of crabs. Most of these hard-shelled creatures live in either deep or shallow water, but a few live on land. Crabs are known for their claws. The size of a crab's claws differs according to its habitat. There are many other differences as well among the crab species. These differences include their texture, their color, and the shapes of their legs, claws, and bodies. Some crabs are excellent swimmers while others run sideways on jointed legs. Crabs feed on other crustaceans, arthropods, and organic matter.

One of the most unusual land crabs is a native of Christmas Island, near Australia. During the rainy season, millions of hand-sized red crabs climb out of their burrows and begin a march to the sea. They cross roads in huge groups, and their sharp claws rip tires like metal spikes. For the people of Christmas Island, this presents a problem. To drive a car in early morning or late evening is to ask for a flat tire. One trucker who had to make an important delivery had 13 punctures!

For most of the year, however, these crabs spend their time in the rain forest. When the dry season approaches, they close their burrows with plugs of dirt and grass in order to keep their gill chambers moist. In the rain forest, the crabs eat leaves, flowers, and other plant parts, leaving the ground relatively free of vegetation. On their trips to the ocean, the crabs eat flowers and grass in people's yards and on the roadsides.

At the end of their long march, the female crabs launch their millions of eggs into the sea. In 25 days, the crabs hatch and color the cliffs a solid, bright red. Soon they begin to move toward the rain forest. They are so tiny that they get into houses under doors and through cracks, and show up on furniture, in cars—everywhere. But Christmas Islanders don't mind, for most of them enjoy the crabs.

Identify the causal relationships in the following sentences. Write *single cause, multiple causes, necessary precondition,* or *no cause-effect* on the lines provided.

1. Millions of crabs must leave their burrows before they can march to the sea.

   _____

2. There are tiny plants growing on the ground. The crabs have food during their trip to the sea.

   _____

3. Crabs have different sizes of claws; crabs have different-shaped bodies.

   _____

4. The claws of the crabs rip holes in tires.

   _____

5. A person lives on Christmas Island and owns a car. She chooses not to drive during certain times of the year.

   _____

6. Why did you choose the answer you selected for question 5?

   _____

7. Crabs must keep their gill chambers moist, so they dig burrows and plug the entrances with dirt and grass.

   _____

8. Crabs must arrive at the sea before the females can launch their eggs into the water.

   _____

9. Match the following causes with their resulting effects. Write the letter of the effect on the right next to its cause on the left.

   _____ Crabs hatch.

   _____ Rains begin.

   _____ Females launch their eggs.

   a. The crabs hatch 25 days later.

   b. Crabs head out to sea.

   c. The cliffs appear bright red.

10. What is the causal relationship in the following? Circle the letter of your answer.

When the dry season approaches, the crabs dig burrows and close them with plugs of dirt and grass.

a. single cause

b. multiple causes

c. necessary precondition

d. no cause-effect

11. Which of the following is a *necessary precondition* for the crabs to go to the sea? Circle the letter of your answer.

a. They cross the road in huge groups.

b. Crabs eat flowers and grass in people's yards.

c. Crabs close their burrows.

d. The rains begin.

12. Why did you choose the answer you selected for question 11?

_____

_____

_____

_____

Workhorses of the Desert

Although camels are thought to have originally lived in North America, today they are found in the deserts of Africa and Asia. They are divided into two main groups: the Arabian camel, which has one hump, and the Bactrian camel, which has two humps.

People have used camels for thousands of years. In the desert, camels are a vital means of transportation for both people and goods. The camel is used in much the same way workhorses are used in the United States. Unlike horses, however, camels are very bad-tempered and dislike working. They will bite humans and animals, including other camels, for no obvious reason. It is very difficult to get them moving, too!

Because of its ability to travel quickly over the shifting sands in the desert and to go for long periods of time with little food or water, the camel is invaluable to many desert people. The notion that camels can go completely without water is a myth, however, as is the belief that they use their humps as storage tanks.

Heavily burdened camels are able to make long trips over deserts because of their economical use of water. They are able to tolerate a greater loss of body water (nearly one third of body weight) than human beings (one eighth of body weight). Camels lose water from their body tissues, leaving the water content of their blood fairly constant. Most mammals lose water from their blood, causing the blood to become sluggish. The blood can then no longer carry away body heat. This leads to heat prostration (symptoms include weakness, dizziness, and nausea), collapse, and possible death.

Camels can consume up to 25 gallons of water in a very short time, taking in as much as they have lost. They thoroughly dilate their body tissues without dying of water intoxication, a condition in which the cells are overly flooded, as would other animals.

Camels can tolerate wide variations in both body fluids and body temperatures. This characteristic further helps them use water economically. The camel's temperature in North Africa can be as low as 93 degrees in the morning and as high as 105 degrees in the afternoon.

To help them survive in the torrid (very hot) deserts of central Asia, India, and North Africa, the camel's metabolic (energy-producing) rate is low, allowing it to live on low-grade, dry food and to get along without water holes for stretches of two weeks or more.

Circle the letter of the best answer to each question.

1. Which of the following statements contains a *necessary precondition?*

   a. The camel's temperature can be 93 degrees in the morning and 105 degrees in the afternoon.

   b. Camels have either one or two humps, and they live in the desert.

   c. Camels are able to travel great distances due to their economical use of water.

2. What is the relationship in the following two sentences? Camels are bad-tempered. Camels have spread throughout the world.

   a. single cause

   b. no cause-effect

   c. multiple causes

   d. necessary precondition

3. What are the three *necessary preconditions* for a camel to be able to exist for long periods of time in the desert? Write your answers on the lines provided.

   a. _____

   b. _____

   c. _____

4. Which of the following statements contains a *necessary precondition?* Circle the letter of your answer.

   a. Camels have been tamed and can be used for transportation.

   b. Camels lived in North America, but there are very few here today.

   c. Camels can make long trips and have nasty tempers.

5. Why did you choose the answer you selected for question 4?

   _____

   _____

   _____

   _____

Identify the causal relationships of the sentences below. Write *single cause, multiple causes, necessary precondition,* or *no cause-effect* on the lines provided.

6. To help it survive in torrid deserts, the camel has a low metabolic rate.

_____

7. Why did you choose the answer you selected for question 6?

_____

8. Camels can consume 25 gallons of water in a short time. Camels can travel long distances between water holes.

_____

9. Camels dislike working. Camels are the workhorses of the desert.

_____

10. Why did you choose the answer you selected for question 9?

_____

_____

_____

11. Camels are mammals. They lose water from their body tissues.

_____

12. Why did you choose the answer you selected for question 11 above?

_____

_____

_____

13. Camels have low metabolic rates. They enjoy eating low-grade, dry food.

_____

14. Why did you choose the answer you selected for question 13?

_____

_____

_____

V.

Open Your Mind and Say "Ahh!":

Understanding the Rules of Rational Thinking

Introduction

If you have ever tried to play checkers or adult card games with preschool children, you know that they really don't care about the rules. They may line the checkers up in a row, or spread the cards all over the floor. This is their idea of an interesting game. It would be enormously frustrating to try to teach them the object, strategies, and rules of play for even one adult table game.

As we grow up in our neighborhoods, schools, and communities, we learn that there are lots of rules that govern our personal conduct, our use of vehicles, our ownership of property, our access to buildings and recreation areas, and even our choices in clothing. Our parents and teachers normally teach us many of these standards and rules.

Some of you may have heard of *Robert's Rules of Order*. These are the guidelines we use for conducting business meetings. We have all heard a presiding officer on a television show say "The meeting will come to order." The person in charge is saying that the group will now be following agreed-upon rules of discussion. The presiding person then serves as a traffic officer. He or she directs the meeting so that members don't get confused and that the group's concerns are given a fair hearing.

Just as there are rules for behavior, there are also rules for rational thinking. These rules are the guidelines that intelligent, thoughtful people follow in developing logically sound conclusions in deliberations. Rational thinking leads to clear discussions and solutions to problems. Nonrational thinking—faulty, unreliable kinds of thinking called *fallacies*—tends to confuse people rather than help them solve problems.

There are many widely recognized fallacies; in this section, we will introduce a dozen. They are divided into three groups of four each. Individuals who use fallacies in their thinking are usually not aware of it. This section will help you recognize faulty reasoning.

Part I

The first four types of faulty reasoning are called the fallacy of *guilt by association*, the fallacy of *appealing to friendship*, the fallacy of *appealing to false pride*, and the fallacy of *false consolation*.

Guilt by Association

In this fallacy, you are known by the company you keep. If your friend has stolen a bicycle, it is assumed that you might do the same. People are suspicious of you because of the reputation your friends have. The fallacy of *guilt by association* assumes that you don't have a mind of your own, and that your friends determine how you will think and act in various situations. In reality, you may have only one or two common interests that you share with your friends; perhaps you are on the same sports team, or you share a favorite hobby. People who see you together, however, may assume that you pattern your life after the others in the group. You can detect the fallacy of guilt by association when someone says, "You can tell what he's like. Look at the people he hangs around with."

Appealing to Friendship

This fallacy rests upon the assumption that if you really like me as a friend, you'll agree with the things I do and say. After all, a true friend doesn't criticize me. A real friend supports me, even when I'm wrong. A trusted friend overlooks my faults and accepts me as I am.

You naturally have to overlook small limitations in friends, but it is wrong to act as though your friends are right in serious matters if they are causing you to give up your own principles of right and wrong. This is too dear a price to pay for friendship. In fact, it might be said that a truly caring friend would not ask you to lie or cover up for him or her. Your friend should honor your right to stand up for things that you feel are just and right. You can detect the fallacy of *appealing to friendship* when you hear someone say, "If you were a real friend, you'd go along with me on this."

Appealing to False Pride

People take great pride in a great many things. Some of these things are worthy of pride; others represent no more than personal power over things or put-downs that make other people feel inferior. If a friend says to you, "Stand up and fight like a man" or "You really told him off," he or she is *appealing to false pride*. If, on the other hand, your friend compliments you for winning an art competition, a debate, or a sports award, or for helping someone who needed assistance, his or her congratulations are focused on achievements that deserve pride. These are accomplishments that require effort and perseverence. You can detect the fallacy of appealing to false pride when people say things like "Show him who's boss" or "Tell her to get lost." These kinds of statements destroy relationships and invite retaliation.

False Consolation

When people use false consolation, they tell you how much worse things could be. If you have a broken leg, they explain that you could be dead. If your puppy dies, they tell you that you could have lost your mother. This is called *false consolation* because it neither recognizes your problem nor makes you feel better. In fact, it simply minimizes or dismisses your problem; you may conclude that you shouldn't have even mentioned it. Your friend has made you feel as if your problem is superficial. You can detect false consolation when someone begins by saying "If you think *you* have a problem . . ." and ends by telling you of people who are much worse off.

Exercise I

Twenty situations are outlined as follows. Write *guilt by association, appealing to friendship, appealing to false pride,* or *false consolation* in the blank beside each situation to identify which fallacy is being used.

_____   1. I know you lost your money and can't go, but at least you aren't crippled or dying.

_____

2. Stay away from Tim's house. His friends may be there, and you know what a bad influence they are on him.

_____

3. Don't worry about the ink on your new blouse. You could have ruined your skirt as well.

_____

4. Tell me the answers. After all, what are buddies for?

_____

5. Alberta will never do her share. The girls she goes around with are real deadbeats.

_____

6. If you cared about me, you'd get the money somehow.

_____

7. If she asks to get into the line, tell her to drop dead.

_____

8. Choose me. I know I didn't try out or practice, but friends should be in the same play.

_____

9. Richard will probably be in jail by the time he's 16. He hangs out with a bunch of troublemakers.

_____

10. You watch the door while I put the watch into my purse. It's the least you can do for a friend.

_____

11. Juan doesn't deserve to be included. Tell him to jump in a lake.

_____

12. A *D* isn't so bad. You could have flunked.

_____

13. Don't let Jane join. Just tell her she's too dumb for our group.

_____

14. Don't let her push you around. Knock her block off.

_____

15. I know you don't have money for your library fine, but at least they won't put you in jail.

_____

16. I wouldn't trust Jim. He hangs around with a bad bunch of kids.

_____   17. I know your mom is really sick, but at least you have your dad at home.

_____   18. Come on, be a real friend. Don't rat on me.

_____   19. Don't invite Maceo to come. He'd probably act like those creeps in his gang.

_____   20. If he tries to get away, show him who's boss.

Part II

The second group of fallacies includes the *strawman technique, rationalization, misuse of humor,* and *gilding the truth.*

Strawman Technique

This is a situation in which a person misrepresents an opponent's position and then tears it apart. It is called the *strawman technique* because the person using it has constructed a cheap imitation of his or her opponent's point of view. It is an exaggeration, a fake. For instance, if your adversary says that she wants to take a look at the possibility of new tax revenues, you say that she plans to spend us into bankruptcy. If she says that she wants to help the poor, you immediately suggest that she wants to set up a lot of giveaway programs. You can detect this kind of fallacy when you hear someone say, "You'll never believe what he's proposing!" Indeed, he'll never believe what you say he is proposing, either.

Rationalization

We have all learned to give excuses when we make mistakes. Psychologists call these excuses *rationalizations*. Excuses, no matter how farfetched they may be, make us feel that we weren't entirely at fault. Rationalizations help convince us, as well as others, that what we did was quite understandable and normal. Rationalizations help protect our feelings of adequacy and competence. If we

throw out valuable belongings with the trash, for example, we explain that the items were so mixed in together that no one could have noticed them. If we break the telephone receiver or a living-room lamp, we may claim that they were not well made and that anyone who used the phone or the lamp would have damaged them. We can detect this kind of fallacy when we hear someone exclaim "I didn't even see it!" or "The thing just broke while I was looking at it."

Misuse of Humor

When people feel that they cannot win an argument by attacking their opponent's position, they may poke fun at the opponent himself or herself. In other words, they try to divert attention from the issue through the use of jokes or humorous references at their opponent's expense. They may suggest that their opponent is not well informed, or, perhaps, downright stupid. "My opponent probably thinks that Sherlock Holmes is a row of houses," they may say. The *misuse of humor* usually begins with something like, "My opponent is so out of touch with what's going on that he thinks . . ."

Gilding the Truth (Using Euphemisms)

People sometimes gloss over a stark problem by using sugar-coated words. For example, if you take a sickly old dog to the veterinarian to have it destroyed, you are likely to say that you had it "put to sleep." It makes you feel better to say it this way.

After all, you don't want to face the fact that you are actually killing the dog. It sounds so harsh and cruel. If you tell someone an outright lie and get caught doing it, you may say that you "stretched the truth a little." You can't deny the lie, but you can make it seem less offensive by describing your action in a mild, offhand manner. You can detect this kind of fallacy when you hear people say things like "It wasn't as bad as you might think. Don't take it so seriously."

Exercise II

Twenty situations are outlined as follows. Write *strawman technique, rationalization, misuse of humor,* or *gilding the truth* in the blank beside each situation to identify which fallacy is being used.

_____ 1. Mrs. Thompson thinks I should do better work, but, after all, nobody can satisfy her.

_____ 2. He looked at my paper a few times during the test, but he really wasn't trying to cheat.

_____ 3. My opponent has such an open mind that if he tips his head sideways, the one idea he has will probably fall out.

_____ 4. Sally took a lipstick from the display in the store. She was just curious about the color.

_____ 5. I know I lost my bike, but it's no big deal. People lose bikes every day.

_____ 6. My opponent wants to put all of the animals in the world on the endangered-species list. Under her plan, we'll be overrun by animals.

_____ 7. Mayor Baker says that the city needs more money. She'll have us all in the poorhouse before she's through.

_____ 8. I wouldn't say my opponent is forgetful, but he does carry a card he can refer to if he forgets his name.

_____ 9. Terry subtracted some points from the other team's score, but she was just careless with her figures.

_____   10. I can't help it if the dish fell and broke. It was slippery because it had soap on it.

_____   11. When the child was taken to the hospital with severe bruises, the mother explained that she was just trying to teach him to be good.

_____   12. My opponent is supposed to be a leader, but he gets lost just trying to find the bathroom.

_____   13. She'll cut back on snow-removal funds. Next winter cars will be stuck in snowdrifts all over town.

_____   14. I know my math isn't finished, but there just wasn't time to do it.

_____   15. Senator Murphy wants more time to consider the bill. We'll all be dead by the time it gets to the Senate floor.

_____   16. Ralph Johnson, my opponent, says he isn't slow, but three snails beat him to the edge of town when he left on vacation.

_____   17. When the dog killed the cat, the dog's owner said that the dog was just playing a little rough.

_____   18. I didn't get a good grade because we weren't given enough time to study.

_____   19. They pick up stray dogs around town. Pretty soon there won't be any dogs left, and no one will have pets.

_____   20. Kendra Johnson says she would like to be county treasurer. I can see why. Nobody else wants to hire her.

Part III

The third group of fallacies includes the *either-or* fallacy, the fallacy of *stipulating a condition that isn't true,* the fallacy of the *slippery slope,* and the fallacy of *procrastination* (foot-dragging).

Either-Or

Suppose someone claims that you must choose between two alternatives because there are, supposedly, no other choices. In almost every situation, however, there are more than two choices; to claim otherwise is to use the *either-or* fallacy. A friend might tell you, "If you don't buy the coat that's on sale in the window, you'll have to wear your old one." It is obvious that there must be other coats. You could buy a coat in a different store, or even borrow one from a friend.

Sometimes either-or fallacies offer two equally uninviting alternatives. "Either we spend money we can't afford on armaments, or we leave ourselves open to certain military attack." This sounds as if we are caught no matter which way we jump, even though other choices exist. For example, we may enter into military agreements with other nations that will give us the protection we need at half the cost. You can detect the either-or fallacy when you hear someone say, "You don't have much choice. Either you do this or you do that."

Stipulating a Condition That Isn't True

We all know people who are wishful thinkers. Instead of facing situations as they really are, they suggest things they *could do* if they only had more money, or more people working on a project, or more time to get the job done, or the special help of an individual with enormous talent. If they just had Michael Jordan on their team, they could win lots of games. If they just had an extra thousand dollars, they could have great decorations for the party.

This kind of wishful thinking presents two problems. It distracts us from getting on with the task at hand, and it may cause us to become dissatisfied with the resources that are actually available to us. At first, the idea of having more money or more time may sound exciting, but *stipulating a condition that isn't true* hardly solves the problem. People who use this fallacy usually begin by saying, "If we only had . . . "

Slippery Slope

The fallacy of the *slippery slope* is so named because once you start down a slippery slope you can't stop. For example, a friend may suggest that you not lend the new boy in class a pencil. "If you lend him a pencil, he'll ask to borrow your ruler next, then your notebook, then . . . " The slippery slope in this case is all the extra borrowing that will follow the first loan. Another friend may caution, "Don't let Sue sit next to you in the cafeteria, because the next thing you know she'll want to sit with you every day. You won't be able to get rid of her." You can detect the fallacy of the slippery slope when you hear people suggest that once you get started in a certain direction, you can never turn back—it will just get worse and worse.

Procrastination (Foot-Dragging)

The fallacy of *procrastination* allows you to agree wholeheartedly with a suggestion or proposal without ever having to help make it happen. When people urge you to support the construction of a community swimming pool, for example, you quickly agree. You may even be a part of the planning. You agree to the size of the pool and the types of equipment that will be needed. You may even suggest ways of financing it, but you do *not* agree to a date for starting the project. This unwillingness to agree to a construction date undermines the whole project. No matter how many details are agreed upon, if the project never begins, there might as well be no plans at all. By procrastinating, you *appear* to be a willing participant, but in reality you are not. Legislators sometimes use the fallacy of procrastination by talking a bill to death in Congress. They say that they want a *good* bill, one that will *really* do the job. In reality, they are just dragging their feet until the bill dies. They keep suggesting new reasons why this is not the time for the project to begin. You can detect this fallacy when you hear someone say, "I agree that this is needed, but, unfortunately, this is not the time to start a project of this nature."

Exercise III

Twenty situations are outlined as follows. Write *either-or, stipulating a condition that isn't true, slippery slope,* or *procrastination* in the blank beside each statement to identify which fallacy is being used.

_____   1. They want the scenery up for the dress rehearsal. We could do a great job if we had more time.

_____   2. If you want to go to the movie, fine. Otherwise, there's nothing to do but stay home.

_____   3. I like the idea a lot. I just don't think we're ready yet to set up a community band.

_____   4. If we lend them money now, they will become dependent on our handouts.

_____   5. If we had more people to help, we could do it in no time.

_____   6. I'd like to see a new city hall, but it's too early to start the project.

_____   7. If we lose the first game, we'll lose our confidence and ruin our chance to win the series.

_____   8. If you don't join the Boys' Club, there won't be anything to do.

_____   9. If one drink will make me feel good, then 10 drinks will make me feel 10 times as good.

_____   10. With two more players, we could have won the game.

_____   11. I'd like to learn to swim. I just don't think I'm ready for lessons right now.

_____   12. You should buy this candy, because there's nothing else you could use the money for.

_____   13. Don't eat that ice cream late at night. Pretty soon you won't be able to go to bed without it.

_____   14. With more money to spend, we could have gone on more rides at the fair.

_____   15. We ought to start a choir. There isn't time or interest on the part of the public right now, however.

_____   16. If you aren't going to help us, you must be against our idea.

_____   17. If I were smarter, I could get all *A*'s.

_____   18. Don't try that expensive shampoo. You'll get used to it and have to have the best of everything from then on.

_____   19. I'm going to exercise regularly. However, I don't feel healthy enough right now.

_____   20. If you don't rank our team as number one, you might as well not rank it at all.

VI.

Too Good to Be True:

Identifying Persuasive Techniques

Introduction

Have you ever heard a statement like this?

"Four out of five doctors who made a choice chose Turtlemeyers Tiny Tablets for stomach upset!"

Of course you have. You hear them all the time, but do you ever stop to think about *what* is being said, and *why?* The "why" part is pretty easy to figure out. The advertiser wants you to buy this product, and he or she is trying to convince you that it is the best product of its type for *you* to purchase.

But *what* is the advertiser saying to convince you? Let's look at the actual words and see what questions we might raise:

"Four out of five doctors . . ."

How many doctors were surveyed? What kind of doctors were they?

If they chose this product, does that necessarily mean I should too?

". . . who made a choice . . ."

How many doctors in the survey *didn't* make a choice?

". . . chose Turtlemeyers . . ."

On what basis did they choose? Did they choose Turtlemeyers because of price? Taste? Effectiveness?

You can see that advertisers don't always tell you everything. But they *do* always appeal to something in you that will make you want to buy the product. In this case, they are appealing to your respect for doctors and your belief that doctors are experts in the use of medicine. The logic goes, "If *doctors* choose this remedy, I should, too.

Advertisers appeal to our most basic interests and desires and concerns in many ways. Here are some of them:

a. They realize that we like to feel important, and that we want to be noticed by others. So, they tell us that their products will make us glamorous, sophisticated, or "macho." We might call this advertising technique **Glamorous You.**

b. They realize that we want to feel confident and proud of our purchases. So, they are careful to tell us that their products are well made, carefully tested, and reliable. Let's call this technique **Top Quality.**

c. They know that we want to get the most for our money. We want to feel like wise shoppers. So, they advertise their products with spectacular sale prices, or claim that they are magnificent bargains. We can call this approach **Great Savings.**

d. They understand that we want to be popular and to be like everyone else. So, they often advertise in a way that makes us think that *everyone* (who is important) has this product; therefore, we should, too. This is often called the **Bandwagon** technique.

e. Sometimes advertisers do just the opposite. They know that sometimes we like to be *exclusive,* to be *different,* to be "the only one" who has a particular product. So, they might appeal to the "snob" in us to get us to buy their product. Let's call this the **Snob Appeal** technique.

f. They have discovered that we are sometimes a little lazy. So, they advertise their products in ways that assure us that they are foolproof and "easy to use." We'll call this technique **Easy to Use.**

g. They know that we often identify with people who are very famous, or who have great prestige in some field. So, they might get glamorous movie stars or well-known sports figures to endorse their products in order to convince us that we too should use them. This is the **Famous Person** technique.

h. Once again, advertisers may do just the opposite, by promoting their product as being for the "common folks," implying that we wouldn't want to use something that only the "rich and famous" use. This advertising technique is often called **Just Plain Folks.**

i. Very clever advertisers have figured out that we like to think of ourselves as kind and considerate. They urge us to buy and give items to others that will truly show that we care—the more expensive the item, the more we care! We'll call this technique **Showing You Care.**

j. Advertisers play on our desires to have, to possess—even if we can't afford—the product. They try to make it appear easy for us to obtain their product through a system of monthly payments or some other special arrangement. They allow us to fulfill our desire to have the product *now.* We'll call this technique **Easy to Own.**

k. Advertisers know that we are very concerned with ourselves, and that we want to think of ourselves as healthy and fit, both physically and mentally. Therefore, they often promote their products as good for our health and well-being. They tell us that by using their product, we are making a wise choice that will make us better people. We'll call this technique **Good for You.**

l. Finally, advertisers sometimes lead us to believe that we will miss an important opportunity if we don't buy their product *right away.* This technique might come in the form of a limited-time offer or an indication that only a very limited quantity of the product is available. The message is that if you don't hurry and purchase the product now, you will not have another chance. In other words, **Don't Get Left Out.**

All of these techniques are commonly used in advertising. Very often, several of them are used within the same advertisement. There is nothing wrong with advertisers using these techniques to convince us to buy their products, unless they actually lie. However, we should be careful not to buy a particular product for the wrong reason. We should be able to recognize these techniques and evaluate whether the product is right for us. The following pages will give you an opportunity to practice recognizing these techniques and thinking clearly about being a wise consumer.

Doll Treasures

Meet Jennifer, an outstanding doll, handcrafted from the finest porcelain. Jennifer is just a few days old and dressed up in her first finery.

Jennifer is the first in a handsome collection of dolls showing the first year of life. She was created by the famous Carleton China Company. Jennifer's head, arms, and legs are hand-cast porcelain, and hand-painted in natural flesh tones. Jennifer's natural sleeping position and soft, cuddly blanket make her perfect to cradle in your arms. The children of seven U.S. presidents have owned and cuddled Carleton China dolls, and now you can, too.

Each doll has the signature of the expert dollmaker. It is hand-numbered and comes with a Certificate of Authenticity. When evaluated against *The Uniform Grading Standards for Dolls*, Jennifer was rated Premier Grade. This rating indicates highest standards of art and craftsmanship, and assures you of an heirloom-quality doll.

Be the proud possessor of this precious doll for only $75.00, an outstanding value for a porcelain doll by an award-winning artist. Hurry! Only a limited number of these precious babies will be issued. Order today!

The persuasive techniques used by advertisers are shown in the large box. Which ones do you think are being used in this ad? In the small boxes below, write the *letter* of each technique you think is used in the ad. On the line beside each box, write some of the words from the ad that illustrate the technique. (You may not need to use all the boxes and lines.)

a. Glamorous You	e. Snob Appeal	i. Showing You Care
b. Top Quality	f. Easy to Use	j. Easy to Own
c. Great Savings	g. Famous Person	k. Good for You
d. Bandwagon	h. Just Plain Folks	l. Don't Get Left Out

☐ _____

☐ _____

☐ _____

☐ _____

☐ _____

Now answer the following questions *based only on this advertisement.*

1. What persuasive technique do you think works *best* in this advertisement? Why?

   _____

   _____

   _____

   _____

   _____

2. What persuasive technique do you think is *least effective* in this advertisement? Why?

   _____

   _____

   _____

   _____

   _____

3. Do you think some other persuasive technique would be effective in advertising this product? Which one? Why would it be effective?

   _____

   _____

   _____

   _____

   _____

4. Assuming you were in the market for a product like this, would you buy this particular one *based on this advertisement*? Why or why not?

   _____

   _____

   _____

   _____

   _____

A Multipurpose Wonder Blender

The same Wonder Blend machine that sold for $119.00 in department stores can now be obtained by direct mail. This is a limited, very special offer—the same Wonder Blend for $19.98.

The Wonder Blend mixes not cream, but skim milk, into a fluffy, tasty topping. Instead of the 300 calories in whipped cream, there are only 40 calories in the Wonder Blend skim milk topping!

But that isn't all. Wonder Blend turns fresh fruit and vegetables into the most delicious, pure, smooth baby food imaginable. It turns peanuts into a creamy, healthful spread.

Use Wonder Blend for milk shakes and for fresh, tangy orange juice. Mix diet drinks in a jiffy. Wonder Blend will whip potatoes, grind meat, and grind coffee. The uses are almost endless.

Each Wonder Blend is backed by a one-year, money-back guarantee.

Orders are limited to two per customer. So hurry and join your friends in experiencing the fun and practicality of owning and using Wonder Blend, the blender for the 21st century.

The persuasive techniques used by advertisers are shown in the large box. Which ones do you think are being used in this ad? In the small boxes below, write the *letter* of each technique you think is used in the ad. On the line beside each box, write some of the words from the ad that illustrate the technique. (You may not need to use all the boxes and lines.)

a. Glamorous You	e. Snob Appeal	i. Showing You Care
b. Top Quality	f. Easy to Use	j. Easy to Own
c. Great Savings	g. Famous Person	k. Good for You
d. Bandwagon	h. Just Plain Folks	l. Don't Get Left Out

☐ _____

☐ _____

☐ _____

☐ _____

☐ _____

Now answer the following questions *based only on this advertisement.*

1. What persuasive technique do you think works *best* in this advertisement? Why?

   _____

   _____

   _____

   _____

   _____

2. What persuasive technique do you think is *least effective* in this advertisement? Why?

   _____

   _____

   _____

   _____

   _____

3. Do you think some other persuasive technique would be effective in advertising this product? Which one? Why would it be effective?

   _____

   _____

   _____

   _____

   _____

4. Assuming you were in the market for a product like this, would you buy this particular one *based on this advertisement*? Why or why not?

   _____

   _____

   _____

   _____

   _____

United States Air Force Jacket

The A-1 Leather Flying Jacket is one of the most important and famous pieces of battle gear in history. During World War II, daring pilots of the United States Air Force relied on the A-1 for protection and comfort. The A-1 was also worn by the "Flying Tigers" in China when they fought in their Warhawks. Jimmy Doolittle's B-25 bomber squadron that hit Tokyo also wore these jackets. Now you can, too! Imagine yourself in one of these stylish leather jackets!

The A-1 jacket is made in the United States of America, using methods called for by the United States Air Force. The premium, hand-stitched goatskin ensures ruggedness and is good-looking. Knitted cuffs and waistband, as well as a cotton-blend lining, provide draft-free comfort. The jacket sports a snap-down collar and large, snap-closed pockets, as well as epaulets.

Own the A-1 Leather Flying Jacket for just $249.00 plus $7.50 for shipping and handling. If you prefer, you may receive the jacket now and pay in six monthly installments of $42.75.

Your satisfaction is guaranteed. If not delighted with your jacket, return it in its original condition within 30 days.

Order today. Available in sizes 34–52, regular and long. Normal delivery for phone orders is four to eight business days.

The persuasive techniques used by advertisers are shown in the large box. Which ones do you think are being used in this ad? In the small boxes below, write the *letter* of each technique you think is used in the ad. On the line beside each box, write some of the words from the ad that illustrate the technique. (You may not need to use all the boxes and lines.)

a. Glamorous You	e. Snob Appeal	i. Showing You Care
b. Top Quality	f. Easy to Use	j. Easy to Own
c. Great Savings	g. Famous Person	k. Good for You
d. Bandwagon	h. Just Plain Folks	l. Don't Get Left Out

Now answer the following questions *based only on this advertisement.*

1. What persuasive technique do you think works *best* in this advertisement? Why?

   _____

   _____

   _____

   _____

   _____

2. What persuasive technique do you think is *least effective* in this advertisement? Why?

   _____

   _____

   _____

   _____

   _____

3. Do you think some other persuasive technique would be effective in advertising this product? Which one? Why would it be effective?

   _____

   _____

   _____

   _____

   _____

4. Assuming you were in the market for a product like this, would you buy this particular one *based on this advertisement*? Why or why not?

   _____

   _____

   _____

   _____

   _____

The Best in the Business

We believe that our agents, the men and women of Service Insurance Agency, rank among the best in the business. They excel in knowledge, experience, and commitment to service. That's why so many of your friends and neighbors in this community have become a part of the Service Insurance Agency family.

The best insurance agents are those dedicated to serving their communities. They are Boy Scout or Girl Scout leaders, Junior Achievement advisors, and members of local community organizations, just like you.

Our agents have invested their lives in their company. When you buy a policy from them, you're putting your trust in an organization that has been a community leader for years. And it is an organization that will get you through tough times. We're on hand when catastrophe strikes.

In short, our agents are there to help plan a secure future for you and your family. We know that when we do business, our reputation is on the line. Our agents are backed up by the best claims adjusters in the industry. Claims are settled quickly, and your check is delivered promptly.

Why not call one of our agents, and do yourself a favor?

The persuasive techniques used by advertisers are shown in the large box. Which ones do you think are being used in this ad? In the small boxes below, write the *letter* of each technique you think is used in the ad. On the line beside each box, write some of the words from the ad that illustrate the technique. (You may not need to use all the boxes and lines.)

a. Glamorous You	e. Snob Appeal	i. Showing You Care
b. Top Quality	f. Easy to Use	j. Easy to Own
c. Great Savings	g. Famous Person	k. Good for You
d. Bandwagon	h. Just Plain Folks	l. Don't Get Left Out

☐ _____

☐ _____

☐ _____

☐ _____

☐ _____

Now answer the following questions *based only on this advertisement.*

1. What persuasive technique do you think works *best* in this advertisement? Why?

   _____

   _____

   _____

   _____

   _____

2. What persuasive technique do you think is *least effective* in this advertisement? Why?

   _____

   _____

   _____

   _____

   _____

3. Do you think some other persuasive technique would be effective in advertising this product? Which one? Why would it be effective?

   _____

   _____

   _____

   _____

   _____

4. Assuming you were in the market for a product like this, would you buy this particular one *based on this advertisement*? Why or why not?

   _____

   _____

   _____

   _____

   _____

ASCOT
Pens

If you're looking for a sensible deal, think ASCOT. Now ASCOT packs a free disposable pen inside your carton when you purchase one dozen ASCOT Ball-Point pens.

ASCOT pens cater to both sides of your brain. It's a super deal for each side. Your logical side will get comfortable, reliable writing from the improved Ball-Point pen. Your creative side will get the smooth-writing Collegiate pen—as a special bonus with your purchase—for expressing your creativity and character.

Both sides will get the satisfaction of using the best pen on the market.

ASCOT Ball-Point and Collegiate pens express high quality in writing materials.

Visit your local stationery store now, since this is a limited-time offer. It's a smart deal for each side of your brain.

The persuasive techniques used by advertisers are shown in the large box. Which ones do you think are being used in this ad? In the small boxes below, write the *letter* of each technique you think is used in the ad. On the line beside each box, write some of the words from the ad that illustrate the technique. (You may not need to use all the boxes and lines.)

a. Glamorous You	e. Snob Appeal	i. Showing You Care
b. Top Quality	f. Easy to Use	j. Easy to Own
c. Great Savings	g. Famous Person	k. Good for You
d. Bandwagon	h. Just Plain Folks	l. Don't Get Left Out

☐ _____

☐ _____

☐ _____

☐ _____

☐ _____

Now answer the following questions *based only on this advertisement.*

1. What persuasive technique do you think works *best* in this advertisement? Why?

   _____

   _____

   _____

   _____

   _____

2. What persuasive technique do you think is *least effective* in this advertisement? Why?

   _____

   _____

   _____

   _____

   _____

3. Do you think some other persuasive technique would be effective in advertising this product? Which one? Why would it be effective?

   _____

   _____

   _____

   _____

   _____

4. Assuming you were in the market for a product like this, would you buy this particular one *based on this advertisement*? Why or why not?

   _____

   _____

   _____

   _____

   _____

Pure Orange Juice Plus

Hi! This is Harvey Wilson, coach of the U.S. Junior Olympics track-and-field team for boys and girls. You know, from the start of those first hungry cries, children steal our hearts, and our energy.

We cuddle, comfort, teach, and guide them. All of this requires real energy on our part. That's where Pure Orange Juice Plus enters the picture. Pure Orange Juice Plus is 100 percent pure orange juice, plus extra nutrition and calcium that helps keep up our health and energy.

Without adequate calcium, our bones can age faster than they should.

The great bonus of Pure Orange Juice Plus is that it provides, ounce for ounce, the same amount of calcium as milk. We get all this, plus the naturally sweet, fresh taste and vitamin C of regular orange juice. It's just what we need to keep every member of the family strong and healthy for years to come.

An eight-ounce glass of Pure Orange Juice Plus provides 30 percent of the U.S. Recommended Daily Allowance of 1,000 milligrams of calcium. Get Pure Orange Juice Plus— because healthy kids need healthy moms and dads.

The persuasive techniques used by advertisers are shown in the large box. Which ones do you think are being used in this ad? In the small boxes below, write the *letter* of each technique you think is used in the ad. On the line beside each box, write some of the words from the ad that illustrate the technique. (You may not need to use all the boxes and lines.)

a. Glamorous You	e. Snob Appeal	i. Showing You Care
b. Top Quality	f. Easy to Use	j. Easy to Own
c. Great Savings	g. Famous Person	k. Good for You
d. Bandwagon	h. Just Plain Folks	l. Don't Get Left Out

☐ _____
☐ _____
☐ _____
☐ _____
☐ _____

Now answer the following questions *based only on this advertisement.*

1. What persuasive technique do you think works *best* in this advertisement? Why?

   _____

   _____

   _____

   _____

2. What persuasive technique do you think is *least effective* in this advertisement? Why?

   _____

   _____

   _____

   _____

3. Do you think some other persuasive technique would be effective in advertising this product? Which one? Why would it be effective?

   _____

   _____

   _____

   _____

4. Assuming you were in the market for a product like this, would you buy this particular one *based on this advertisement*? Why or why not?

   _____

   _____

   _____

   _____

VII.

The Writer Behind the Writing:

Recognizing the Writer's Assumptions

Introduction

Suppose one of your friends stops you in the hall at school to say, "Hey, I've got some of my allowance left this week. Come with me to the ice cream shop after school, and I'll buy you one of Shorty's famous shakes."

"No thanks," you reply. "I'll come with you, but I don't want you to buy me a shake."

"What's the matter?" your friend asks. "Are you too proud? I thought we were friends, and I like to do things for my friends."

"Oh, it's not that," you say. "It's just that I don't like ice cream."

"You what?!"

As unlikely as this story might be, it does illustrate something that very often happens in communication—making assumptions. When we *assume,* we take something for granted. We consider something to be true without stopping to make sure. In this case, your friend assumed you liked ice cream. He never thought to stop and check this out. In fact, this was probably a pretty safe assumption. Most people *do* like ice cream.

When we're reading, however, it is often important to be aware of assumptions that writers may be making. These assumptions may not always be obvious on the surface. For example, consider this statement: "After algebra this semester, Jim will have only one more math class to take." The assumption being made here is that Jim will *pass* his current algebra class.

What assumption is being made in this statement: "The allied victory in this war will finally bring peace to this troubled region of the world"?

The writer is assuming that

   a. the war is about over,

   b. this region of the world is usually peaceful,

   c. the allies will win the war.

If you chose *c,* you're right. The writer assumes that the allies will win.

As readers, we must recognize a writer's assumptions in order to discover and analyze those assumptions that might be faulty or might lead to wrong conclusions. Although there is no way to guarantee that we will always do this effectively, there are some habits we can develop to recognize a writer's assumptions.

1. Be sure you know what the writer has actually *said*. What statements or conclusions does the writer make?

2. Ask yourself "Are these statements or conclusions clearly based on information the writer has provided, or is he or she making some assumptions?"

3. If assumptions are being made, are they justified? Are they assumptions that you can accept? Are they critical to understanding or accepting the author's information?

The following exercises will help you to practice the art of recognizing and evaluating writers' assumptions.

Raising Fuel Standards

Once again the cry for fuel economy has picked up steam. Rising prices at the gas pump have made gas guzzlers somewhat less desirable. No immediate prospects for cheaper fuel seem to be at hand.

One way to cut down on the need for expensive oil is to make cars more fuel-efficient. Auto companies have made gains in fuel efficiency in the past, but when gasoline prices drop, customers ask for bigger cars again.

Since 1975, auto manufacturers have doubled the fuel economy of compact cars to 27.5 miles per gallon, with no loss of performance or interior room. However, auto industry defenders claim that it is impossible to make cars that are even more fuel-efficient. They say it is too costly to retool and that jobs will be lost. Also, they maintain that mid- and large-sized cars are safer.

According to a recent study by Marc Ledbetter of the American Council of an Energy Efficient Economy and Max Ross of the University of Michigan Department of Physics, there are 17 different technological wonders that, if used more widely, would raise average mileage to 43.8 miles per gallon without changing car size or performance. If that is true, we could save 2,800,000 barrels of oil a day. That is about 45 percent of the oil we use for cars. This savings would go a long way toward keeping our lungs and lives free of oil abuse.

Answer the following questions about assumptions.

1. What assumption does the writer appear to be making about people in general? Circle your choice.

   a. That they are not concerned about saving fuel

   b. That they are uninformed about the possibilities of saving fuel

   c. That they would buy more fuel-efficient cars if they were given the choice

2. Do you think the writer of this article is making the following assumptions? Check "Yes" or "No" and briefly indicate what in the article helped you decide. If you check "Yes," then tell whether you think the assumption is justified, and why.

   a. *Automakers will always use the best technology available.*

   Is the writer making this assumption? Yes ☐ No ☐

   What in the article helped you decide? _____

   _____

If you answered "Yes," do you think this assumption is justified?   Yes ☐   No ☐

Why or why not? _____

_____

b. *The supply of oil is limited.*

Is the writer making this assumption?   Yes ☐   No ☐

What in the article helped you decide? _____

_____

If you answered "Yes," do you think this assumption is justified?   Yes ☐   No ☐

Why or why not? _____

_____

c. *Auto manufacturers are more interested in profits than in the public good.*

Is the writer making this assumption?   Yes ☐   No ☐

What in the article helped you decide? _____

_____

If you answered "Yes," do you think this assumption is justified?   Yes ☐   No ☐

Why or why not? _____

_____

d. *People in this country drive too much.*

Is the writer making this assumption?   Yes ☐   No ☐

What in the article helped you decide? _____

_____

If you answered "Yes," do you think this assumption is justified?   Yes ☐   No ☐

Why or why not? _____

_____

3. What other assumption(s) does the writer appear to be making about the study by Ledbetter and Ross?

   _____

   _____

   _____

   _____

   _____

   _____

4. Based on your examination of the writer's assumptions, what would you say about this article? Check the box before the response that comes closest to your analysis.

   ☐ Sounds OK to me. The writer stayed on solid ground.

   ☐ It's probably OK. The writer made *some* unjustified assumptions, but they were minor.

   ☐ I reject it. The writer bases too much of what is said on assumptions that cannot be justified.

Misery Brings Success

If a person is overweight, he or she should ignore all the diet books. No matter how popular the book becomes, it is usually a rip-off. Each author of a weight-loss book tries to convince people that they can eat yummy food and lose weight. These books use such teasers as the eat-anything-you-want title and the three-squares-a-day reducing method.

No matter how enticing the title, in the end the only diet that works is the you-gotta-suffer diet. All you have to do is follow one simple rule: If you like and enjoy it, you can't have it; if you hate it, eat lots of it.

If you go to a restaurant, order broiled whitefish or baked halibut with sliced tomatoes—no sauce or other trimmings. As for your drink, limit it to water, or possibly a diet soda. For dessert choose a sherbet, or perhaps a melon slice. For breakfast, eat a bowl of oatmeal and drink the juice of fresh fruit. If you must snack, choose low-fat yogurt.

Stick to these rules day and night, for meals and snacks. This diet doesn't sound as good as some of those others, but it will work. And when the fat melts away, just think how noble you will feel.

1. What assumption about people is the writer of this article making? Circle the letter of your choice.

   a. That people have tried several diets

   b. That people are all overweight

   c. That people who are overweight don't want to be that way

2. Do you think the writer of this article is making the following assumptions? Check "Yes" or "No" and briefly indicate what in the article helped you decide. If you checked "Yes," then tell whether you think the assumption is justified, and why.

   a. *Foods cannot be tasty and low in calories at the same time.*

      Is the writer making this assumption?   Yes ☐   No ☐

      What in the article helped you decide? _____

      _____

      If you answered "Yes," do you think this   Yes ☐   No ☐
      assumption is justified?

      Why or why not? _____

      _____

b. *It is impossible to eat out and stay on a diet.*

Is the writer making this assumption?   Yes ☐   No ☐

What in the article helped you decide? _____

_____

If you answered "Yes," do you think this assumption is   Yes ☐   No ☐
justified?

Why or why not? _____

_____

c. *Following the "one simple rule" will definitely result in weight loss.*

Is the writer making this assumption?   Yes ☐   No ☐

What in the article helped you decide? _____

_____

If you answered "Yes," do you think this assumption is   Yes ☐   No ☐
justified?

Why or why not? _____

_____

d. *Our body weight is related to how good we feel about ourselves.*

Is the writer making this assumption?   Yes ☐   No ☐

What in the article helped you decide? _____

_____

If you answered "Yes," do you think this assumption is   Yes ☐   No ☐
justified?

Why or why not? _____

_____

3. What assumption(s) does the writer appear to be making about the people who write "popular" diet books?

_____

_____

_____

_____

_____

_____

_____

_____

_____

_____

4. Based on your examination of the writer's assumptions, what would you say about this article?

☐ Sounds OK to me. The writer stayed on solid ground.

☐ It's probably OK. The writer made *some* unjustified assumptions, but they were minor.

☐ I reject it. The writer bases too much of what is said on assumptions that cannot be justified.

Exploring the Jungles of Africa

Dr. David Livingstone opened up more of the world's unexplored landmasses than any other person in history. His life stands as a model of courage and tenacity. Livingstone's amazing success was due to his strong religious beliefs, his urge to help sick people, and his pleasant personal manners. He always treated strangers as friends and brothers.

Livingstone was born in 1813, in Blantyre, Scotland. When he reached the age of 10, his parents sent him to work in the local spinning mills. He chose to work 12 hours a day so that he could afford to go to medical school in Glasgow. He wanted to become a medical missionary. In 1840, at the age of 27, he joined the missionary society and set out for Africa. Livingstone helped to establish Christian missions and provide medical assistance in areas where no Europeans had gone before.

Livingstone's dream involved an enormous number of risks and dangers. He and his men faced impenetrable jungles, strange diseases, warlike tribes, and ferocious animals. Livingstone had no maps, no radios, and no rescue teams that he could call on in an emergency. People outside Africa didn't even know where he was. Although he had medicines, these were very crude and limited. There were no antibiotics or even anesthetics to use during surgery; they were not in use yet. He and his team often suffered from malaria and dysentery.

It is difficult for us today to really understand how dedicated and persistent Livingstone was. He wanted to see all of Africa from the Atlantic coast to the Indian Ocean. His discovery of the Zambezi River in 1851 seemed to be the turning point in his explorations. This river runs halfway across the center of Africa from west to east. It made travel across the continent much easier.

Livingstone traveled thousands of miles back and forth across Africa with his medicine chest, his Bible, and his "magic lantern," a simple slide projector, which he used to illustrate his missionary lectures. As a result of these ventures into the unknown, Livingstone gave the world five priceless gifts:

1. He offered the world its first intelligent and sympathetic view of African cultures. Up until his time, Europeans saw Africans as oddities, people with strange customs and inferior standards of behavior.

2. Secondly, Livingstone emphasized the horrors of the slave trade run by the Arabs and the Portuguese. His reports helped prompt European leaders to terminate this trade in human suffering.

3. Thirdly, Livingstone made careful maps and charts of all the regions he visited. These were copied by the Royal Geographical Society in London and made available to future travelers to the continent.

4. Fourthly, he described and documented many of the strange diseases he observed. He also listed possible preventions and cures.

5. Finally, Livingstone reported on various resources—minerals, plants, and animals—that might offer additional sources of income for Africans.

   The Africans truly appreciated the enormous contributions of Dr. Livingstone.

When he died in a small village near the upper waters of the Nile River, Africans came by the thousands to pay their last respects. His personal servants, Susi and Chuma, knew that the doctor's own people would want his body for burial. First, however, they removed his heart and buried it where it belonged, in the soil of his beloved Africa. Dr. Livingstone's body rests today in the great cathedral of Westminster Abbey in England.

Respond to the following questions as directed.

1. What assumptions does the writer appear to be making about a person's success and his or her pleasant manners? Circle the letter of your choice.

   a. Pleasant manners help, but they don't make a lot of difference.

   b. Pleasant manners can make a great difference in the success of an operation.

   c. Pleasant manners are likely to be harmful because people take advantage of you.

2. Do you think the writer of this article is making the following assumptions? Check "Yes" or "No." Then briefly tell what in the article helped you decide.

   a. *Livingstone was unusually brave.*

      Is the writer making this assumption?   Yes ☐   No ☐

      What in the article helped you decide? _____

      _____

   b. *Livingstone was very intelligent.*

      Is the writer making this assumption?   Yes ☐   No ☐

      What in the article helped you decide? _____

      _____

c. *Livingstone wanted to help other people even after his own death.*

Is the writer making this assumption?   Yes ☐   No ☐

What in the article helped you decide? _____

_____

d. *Livingstone cared very deeply about people.*

Is the writer making this assumption?   Yes ☐   No ☐

What in the article helped you decide? _____

_____

e. *Livingstone was very curious and inquisitive about people and nature.*

Is the writer making this assumption?   Yes ☐   No ☐

What in the article helped you decide? _____

_____

f. *Livingstone was very confident and resourceful.*

Is the writer making this assumption?   Yes ☐   No ☐

What in the article helped you decide? _____

_____

g. *Livingstone was more attached to Africa than he was to Scotland, where he was born.*

Is the writer making this assumption?   Yes ☐   No ☐

What in the article helped you decide? _____

_____

h. *Livingstone thought it was important to tell people about Christianity.*

Is the writer making this assumption?   Yes ☐   No ☐

What in the article helped you decide? _____

_____

The Stories Behind Cave Paintings

A nine-year-old Spanish girl named María de Sautuola was hiking with her father near the Altamira Caves in northern Spain 100 years ago. Like so many children her age, the caverns fascinated her. They looked dark and dangerous but inviting at the same time. María ducked into one cavern after another. Suddenly, she screamed, "Bulls! Bulls!" Her father, fearful and trembling, raced into the darkened grotto. María pointed to the ceiling. There, spread across the ceiling of the cave, were beautifully painted outlines of prehistoric bison. They were magnificent works of art created by Cro-Magnon people more than 15,000 years ago.

The 17 bison on the ceiling of the cave were not just stick figures. They were depicted in lifelike poses: lying down, pawing the ground, bellowing, and dying from spear wounds. Around this herd of bison, there were sketches of a wolf, a boar, a deer, and a horse. A little later, María and her father discovered dozens of other paintings farther inside the cavern. These paintings showed several prehistoric animals that had disappeared from western Europe thousands of years before.

Most archeologists (scientists who study prehistoric cultures) thought that the cave drawings in Spain were fakes. They suggested that our early ancestors were little more than savages, similar to the apes of their day. Such people couldn't possibly have created such magnificent pictures. The archeologists concluded that a talented trickster had sketched the animals as a way of fooling gullible visitors.

Finally, three decades later, an archeologist named Abbé Henri Breuil examined the caves at Altamira and unearthed animal bones with engravings on them very similar to those on the ceilings. The doubters and critics were quickly convinced. Our ancestors really were talented! Even though they lived during the Stone Age, their engravings were breathtaking.

In 1940, an 18-year-old boy, Marcel Ravidat, took three friends to a hole in the side of a hill near Lascaux, France. A tree had fallen and unearthed an underground tunnel. Marcel and his friends dropped 18 feet to the floor of the cavern. They struck a few matches and discovered animal paintings on the walls. The boys reported their findings to Abbé Breuil who soon found sketches of horses and deer in nearby caverns. Altogether, more than 100 grottoes decorated with drawings and paintings have been found throughout southern France and northern Spain.

The cave paintings at Altamira, Spain, remain the most vivid and colorful of the grotto drawings. The artists created black paints from charcoal, and they developed red, yellow, and orange hues from iron oxides. The temperature and humidity in these caves remained constant over the years, so the colors did not dry out and scale off the ceilings.

Archeologists have offered various theories regarding the creation of cave art. Some think that early people may have believed that the cave drawings would cast a spell over the beasts they were attempting to slay. Some archeologists think that the early people were trying to acquire some of the strength and swiftness of their prey. Still other scientists speculate that these drawings could have been used to instruct new hunters in the techniques of killing wild game. Regardless of the reasons for the art, archeologists have been amazed that our ancestors were so gifted and talented.

Answer the following questions about assumptions.

1. What important assumption is this article based on? Circle the letter of your choice.

    a. Cave art can tell us a great deal about the lives of early people.

    b. There were talented artists during the early years of human existence.

    c. People lived in caves during prehistoric times.

2. Do you think the writer of this article is making the following assumptions? Check "Yes" or "No." Then tell what in the article helped you decide.

    a. *Scientists are very careful in drawing conclusions about things they observe.*

    Is the writer making this assumption?   Yes☐   No☐

    What in the article helped you decide? _____

    _____

    b. *Archeologists are curious about why early people acted in specific ways.*

    Is the writer making this assumption?   Yes☐   No☐

    What in the article helped you decide? _____

    _____

    c. *Archeologists are very careful observers.*

    Is the writer making this assumption?   Yes☐   No☐

    What in the article helped you decide? _____

    _____

d. *Archeologists sometimes can only speculate about the reasons early people acted in certain ways.*

Is the writer making this assumption?   Yes ☐   No ☐

What in the article helped you decide? _____

_____

e. *Archeologists know about animals that have disappeared from the face of the earth.*

Is the writer making this assumption?   Yes ☐   No ☐

What in the article helped you decide? _____

_____

f. *Archeologists generally work at a very slow pace.*

Is the writer making this assumption?   Yes ☐   No ☐

What in the article helped you decide? _____

_____

g. *The cave art is clearly worth preserving.*

Is the writer making this assumption?   Yes ☐   No ☐

What in the article helped you decide? _____

_____

Keeping Kids Healthy

We know that physical activity can help fight diseases, from cancer to mental illness. It can improve self-image and raise energy levels, among other things. So it is not hard to see that the future of our nation depends on a society that is fit and healthy, physically and mentally.

Well, how are we doing? Many people would say not very well. It sometimes seems that the heaviest exercise our children get is raising a piece of pizza from the table to their mouths. A recent, wide-ranging study, however, showed that two thirds of children between the ages of 10 and 17 do get enough exercise to maintain cardiovascular fitness (fitness that involves the heart and blood vessels). However, only one eighth of adults get this much exercise.

The problem is that this fitness in children doesn't last. In physical education classes, only about one fourth of the children's time is spent in actual activity. An equal amount of time is spent just waiting. Furthermore, less than half of the time spent in physical activity is used for the kinds of activity that the children can use for a lifetime, such as jogging, swimming, or bicycling.

We need to change the way we teach physical fitness in the schools. Only in this way will we meet the challenge of becoming a physically fit nation.

Answer the following questions about assumptions.

1. What assumption about people in general does the writer of this article seem to be making? Circle your choice.

   a. That they are not aware of the important facts about fitness

   b. That they don't care about fitness

   c. That they are already physically fit

2. Do you think the writer of this article is making the following assumptions? Check "Yes" or "No" and briefly indicate what in the article helped you decide. If you checked "Yes," then tell whether you think the assumption is justified, and why.

   a. *Children's physical fitness is a direct result of what we teach in physical education classes.*

   Is the writer making this assumption?   Yes ☐   No ☐

   What in the article helped you decide? _____

   _____

If you answered "Yes," do you think this assumption is justified?   Yes ☐   No ☐

Why or why not? _____

_____

b. *The majority of time in physical education classes ought to be spent in actual physical activities.*

Is the writer making this assumption?   Yes ☐   No ☐

What in the article helped you decide? _____

_____

If you answered "Yes," do you think this assumption is justified?   Yes ☐   No ☐

Why or why not? _____

_____

c. *Improving the fitness of children will cause an improvement in the fitness of adults.*

Is the writer making this assumption?   Yes ☐   No ☐

What in the article helped you decide? _____

_____

If you answered "Yes," do you think this assumption is justified?   Yes ☐   No ☐

Why or why not? _____

_____

d. *The benefits of good physical fitness are worth the effort.*

Is the writer making this assumption?   Yes ☐   No ☐

What in the article helped you decide? _____

_____

If you answered "Yes," do you think this assumption is justified?   Yes ☐   No ☐

Why or why not? _____

_____

3. What assumption(s) do you think the writer might be making about the people who would read this article?

_____

_____

_____

_____

_____

_____

_____

_____

_____

4. Based on your examination of the writer's assumptions, what would you say about this article? Check the box before the response that comes closest to your analysis.

☐ Sounds OK to me. The writer stayed on solid ground.

☐ It's probably OK. The writer made *some* unjustified assumptions, but they were minor.

☐ I reject it. The writer bases too much of what is said on assumptions that cannot be justified.

Too Many Starlings?

To the Editor:

As a federally and state-licensed migratory-bird rehabilitator, one who nurses injured birds back to health, I was dismayed by "100 Years of the Starling." Theodore Lafeber, a pioneer in avian (bird) medicine, said that if pigeons were as dangerous to human health as has often been stated, cities would be without people. The same holds true for starlings.

True, starlings do cause problems, but they are only one of many problems facing us. In fact, starlings make lovely, affectionate pets. They speak like parrots, only clearer.

Some years ago, Searle Laboratories developed Ornithol, a pigeon birth control. Given twice a day for 10 days, it reduces flocks by 75 percent in 18 months with no killing. The eggs simply do not hatch. If we can put people on the moon, we can develop a birth control for starlings. However, such ideas do not appeal to pest-control companies.

I would work as hard to save a starling as any other bird, since to me all life is irreplaceable. We need to remember that starlings have been here for a long time—longer than the families of many people making their homes here now.

In time, history will judge us by how we treat those unable to protect themselves from our conduct and our laws.

Answer the following questions about assumptions.

1. What assumption does the writer of this article make about the people who read this letter to the editor? Circle your choice.

   a. That they don't like starlings

   b. That they know all about starlings

   c. That they have read "100 Years of the Starling"

2. Do you think the writer of this article is making the following assumptions? Check "Yes" or "No," and briefly indicate what in the article helped you decide. If you checked "Yes," then tell whether you think the assumption is justified, and why.

   a. *We have no right to control the size of the starling population.*

   Is the writer making this assumption?   Yes ☐   No ☐

   What in the article helped you decide? _____

   _____

If you answered "Yes," do you think this assumption is justified?   Yes ☐   No ☐

Why or why not? _____

_____

b. *Preventing eggs from hatching would be more humane than killing birds after they are hatched.*

Is the writer making this assumption?   Yes ☐   No ☐

What in the article helped you decide? _____

_____

If you answered "Yes," do you think this assumption is justified?   Yes ☐   No ☐

Why or why not? _____

_____

c. *Development of a birth-control method for starlings is highly unlikely.*

Is the writer making this assumption?   Yes ☐   No ☐

What in the article helped you decide? _____

_____

If you answered "Yes," do you think this assumption is justified?   Yes ☐   No ☐

Why or why not? _____

_____

d. *The fact that starlings have been in the United States for a long time gives them some special rights.*

Is the writer making this assumption?   Yes ☐   No ☐

What in the article helped you decide? _____

_____

If you answered "Yes," do you think this assumption is justified?   Yes ☐   No ☐

Why or why not? _____

_____

3. What assumption(s) does the writer appear to be making about pest-control companies?

_____

_____

_____

_____

_____

_____

_____

_____

_____

4. Based on your examination of the writer's assumptions, what would you say about this article? Check the box before the response that is closest to your analysis.

☐ Sounds OK to me. The writer stayed on solid ground.

☐ It's probably OK. The writer made *some* unjustified assumptions, but they were minor.

☐ I reject it. The writer bases too much of what is said on assumptions that cannot be justified.

Answer Key

I. Getting to the Heart of the Matter: Judging the Relevance of Information for Specific Purposes

Introduction

1. NO	5. YES
2. NO	6. NO
3. YES	7. NO
4. NO	

The Statue of Liberty

1. a	6. b
2. b	7. a
3. c	8. c
4. c	9. a
5. a	10. c

Developing the Parachute

1. d	6. b
2. c	7. a
3. c	8. b
4. c	9. b
5. d	10. c

The Polar Bear's World

1. a	6. a
2. b	7. b
3. b	8. a
4. c	9. c
5. b	10. a

Across the Atlantic in a Sailboat

1. b	6. b
2. a	7. d
3. b	8. a
4. d	9. d
5. c	10. a

As Warm as Ice

1. c	6. a
2. b	7. b
3. b	8. b
4. b	9. a
5. b	10. c

Message in a Bottle

1. b	6. b
2. c	7. c
3. b	8. a
4. b	9. c
5. b	10. b

The Amazing Dolphins

1. c	6. b
2. c	7. c
3. c	8. a
4. a	9. b
5. a	10. d

Follow-up Activities

1. Challenge students to list sources of information on a topic such as "How to Sail a Boat." (Sources could include experts, sailing manuals, reference books, or web sites.)

2. Ask pupils to enumerate the relevant information they would need to build a doghouse. (Relevant information includes materials needed, tools needed, dimensions, and size of the dog.)

3. Read aloud an ad from the local newspaper about a lost pet, but leave out several details. Ask students to suggest relevant information that would help in the recovery of the animal (locations, color, breed, name it answers to, and so on).

4. Bring in a variety of publications (such as a *Farmer's Almanac, Sports Illustrated,* JCPenney's catalog, *Boys' Life, Roget's Thesaurus,* an atlas) and match topics to the most relevant source.

5. Have groups of pupils act out a conversation in which two students contribute relevant ideas and suggestions while a third student adds only irrelevant information.

6. Assume that you would like to keep a burro at your home. What information would be most relevant? (Relevant information includes local laws, costs, care of the animal when you are away, required vaccinations, suitability of the environment for the animal, and so on.)

II. Just the Facts, Ma'am: Distinguishing Among Facts, Assumptions, and Values

Introduction

1. fact
2. assumption
3. value statement
4. fact
5. assumption
6. fact
7. value statement
8. assumption
9. value statement
10. fact

Who Has the Right to Decide?

1. fact
2. fact
3. value statement
4. fact
5. value statement
6. value statement
7. a
8. The judge gave Mrs. Cheng two months to prove that non-Western methods were effective.
9. c
10. The Supreme Court required a Laotian family to submit their child for surgery even though it was against their beliefs.

Strange Ways of Predicting the Future

I. 1. fact
    2. value statement
    3. assumption
    4. fact
    5. value statement
    6. assumption
    7. value statement
II. a
III. Only *a* is not shown in the article.
IV. 1. assumption
    2. value statement
    3. fact
    4. value statement
    5. assumption
    6. assumption
    7. fact
V. Answers will vary.

To the North Pole

1. fact
2. fact
3. value statement
4. fact
5. assumption
6. value statement
7. assumption
8. d
9. Penguins are not found at the North Pole, and they do not affect the trip in any way.
10. 5, 4, 2, 3, 7, 1, 6
11. Without perseverance, the person could not finish the trip.
12. Saving money is not related to this trip.

(Answers to 10, 11, and 12 may vary.)

Chief of the Eel River Tribes

1. fact
2. value statement
3. assumption
4. value statement
5. value statement
6. fact
7. assumption
8. a, b, d, g
9. a, b, c, g
10. Little Turtle was very willing to try new things—vaccinations and farming, for example.

(Answers to 8, 9, and 10 may vary.)

Caring for Our Animal Friends

1. fact
2. value statement
3. value statement
4. fact
5. fact
6. assumption
7. assumption
8. a, c
9. a, b, c, f, g
10. Some animal-management specialists believe that medical care weakens an animal's natural defenses against disease.

She Chose Freedom

1. fact
2. value statement
3. fact
4. assumption
5. value statement
6. assumption
7. fact
8. a, b, c, e
9. c
10. You can make up for time or money that you give away, but you have only one life to give. A person who risks her life risks the ultimate sacrifice.

    (Answers to 9 and 10 may vary.)

Busy Builders

1. c, d, e, f
2. c. Animal activists' biggest concern is protecting animals from harm and suffering.
3. a, c, d, e
4. c. Wildlife damage control officers are responsible for protecting property, especially valuable property.

Follow-up Activities

1. Choose a topic for a class newsletter. One group should write an editorial expressing opinions about the topic. Other groups should collect factual information and write a news article about the topic.

2. Write a series of factual statements and opinions on the board. See if students can change opinions to factual statements and factual statements to opinions. For example: "Dogs make the best pets" could be changed to "Al likes dogs."

3. Have students read short biographies and discuss the values that are most apparent in the lives of the main characters.

4. Challenge students to list the values that should be emphasized in giving sports awards. For example, should personal effort be valued over playing fairly? Should improvement be valued over high scores?

5. Encourage pupils to write radio or television commercials. Have them underline the facts and circle the assumptions in their commercials.

6. Ask each member of the class to bring in one or two very short newspaper clippings that propose some course of action. See if the students can differentiate between those proposals that are for the common good and those that represent selfish interests.

7. Divide the class into groups of two or three for a role-playing activity. One student takes the role of a person new to town. The other student or students are helpful passersby. The newcomer student asks the resident(s) for help (directions, a restaurant recommendation, and so on). Ask students to develop a dialogue in which the residents make incorrect assumptions about what the newcomer knows or wants.

III. Who, What, Where, When, Why, and How: Understanding How Conditions or Events in a Story or Report Relate to Each Other

The Black Death

I. 1. They burned the clothes and belongings of people who had died of the disease; they burned cats, dogs, rats, and mice; they wore flowers to ward off evil spirits.
   2. The fire eliminated unsanitary conditions that had helped to spread the plague.
   3. The disease is easily transmitted.

II. 1. Answers will vary.
2. Answers will vary.

The Spy Who Came in From the Sea

1. The British wanted to plant the idea that the information was very important.
2. Since Spain was sympathetic to the enemy, intelligence officials believed that the Spanish would turn over the information to its intended audience.
3. Answers will vary.
4. The assumption is that the undercover people would be accepted and not suspected.
5. Answers will vary.

Gifts From Outer Space

1. We use satellites for transmitting information, images, and rock concerts.
2. We use sensors on the skin to record body functions. We use a system for checking on cars that is similar to the system that monitors a space capsule.
3. Scientists developed cushioned soles for tennis shoes from clothing prepared for astronauts. Researchers also used lightweight materials from rocket motors to develop breathing equipment for firefighters.

Capping the Devil's Cigarette Lighter

1. At first, there was no fire at the well. Later, when the fire spread to the derrick over the well, they needed the best help they could get.
2. Red Adair used explosives to cut off oxygen from the fire so it couldn't burn.
3. If he had planted the explosives in the area while it was hot, they might have gone off immediately, killing Adair before he could escape.
4. The derrick was above the hole where he planned to place the explosives. The damaged parts had to be removed so they wouldn't fall on him while he was doing his job.

Fearless Travels into the Unknown

I. 1. Some hardships are listed: frozen mountain ranges, wild animals, bandits, scorching deserts, blinding sandstorms, illness.
2. He may have been more famous because he wrote the book.
3. This made the journey more exciting and interesting, both to the travelers and to those who read of them.
4. The emperor gave him the run of the palaces and summer resorts and took him on personal trips. He also made Marco Polo his personal emissary.
5. Answers will vary.

II. 1. He wrote an inspiring book about his positive experiences.
2. It inspired Columbus not to do exactly the same thing but to explore unknown places.
3. Answers will vary.

Counting Animal Populations

1. Large animals that are hard to run down; birds that are hard to capture because they can fly
2. It is a check on endangered species. It provides a picture of future food supplies.
3. Multiplying the number of animals in one area by the number of similar areas in the world gives an estimate of the total number of specimens in the world.
4. That specimens are equally distributed throughout the world

The Chisholm Trail

1. Texas ranchers were eager to get their cattle to the East, where they would sell for much more money.
2. The trail made large quantities of meat available at low prices, so more people could afford to add meat to their diets.
3. The trail did not have an asphalt surface and lines like our highways; cattle could easily roam off the beaten track.
4. They could string barbed wire around their fields to protect their crops from cattle.

Europe's Mystery People

1. They were vulnerable to invasion and were conquered several times.

2. They carried on 80 percent of the shipping with the Americas during the sixteenth century; when they moved to Uruguay and Argentina, they became shepherds.

3. By practicing transhumance, the Basques were able to find better pastures for their sheep and thus have better herds.

4. A growing interest in Basque culture

Follow-up Activities

1. Discuss a story set in the present day. Ask pupils how the plot, setting, and characters would change if the story took place 200 years ago.

2. Read a short story to the class. Then ask the students to rank the importance of the setting, the plot, the characters, and the style. In some stories, the setting is crucial because it tells about life in a strange land. In other stories, the main character is what is interesting in the story. Ask students to explain their rankings.

3. Help the class write a story that describes a main character in a serious conflict. Include descriptions of the character's reactions to the conflict. Then challenge the students to write a profile of the main character, explaining what he or she is like.

4. Ask a group of students to rewrite a familiar story in a different style. For example, "The Three Little Pigs" could be rewritten as a police report.

5. Fables and folktales normally contain a moral lesson. Challenge the class to rewrite an animal story so that it becomes a fable.

6. Have three baskets with slips of paper in each basket. The first basket has characters' names written on the slips, the second basket has plots, and the third basket has settings. Have students draw one slip from each basket and write a short story.

IV. Why the Chicken Crossed the Road: Recognizing Cause-Effect Relationships

Introduction

I. c, d, f, g

II. c, d, f, g, h

III. a, b, c, f, h

Magicians and Escape Artists

1. a, b
2. c, b, a
3. c
4. d
5. a
6. c
7. They had to cover up the evidence, or people would know the box had been opened.
8. a, c
9. In *a,* two things caused him to become famous; in *c,* two things contributed to the clapping.
10. no cause-effect
11. multiple causes
12. single cause
13. Lowering him into the water was the single factor that cut off his supply of air and light.

An Unbelievable Ride to Victory

1. a
2. a
3. c
4. d
5. d
6. a
7. d
8. b
9. d
10. b

Rescue of the USS S-5

1. single cause
2. necessary precondition
3. single cause
4. multiple cause
5. no cause-effect
6. a, d
7. b, c, a
8. air valve was left open; single cause
9. a

10. a, c, d
11. a

Making the World Safe for All Living Things

1. a
2. b
3. a, b
4. You need a lot of land to provide animals with a natural habitat, and all this land and care cost a great deal of money.
5. a. single cause
   b. no cause-effect
   c. necessary precondition
   d. multiple causes
   e. no cause-effect
   f. necessary precondition
   g. multiple causes
   h. multiple causes

Clever but Deadly

1. single cause
2. no cause-effect
3. single cause
4. no cause-effect
5. necessary precondition
6. eight legs, no antennae, no wings
7. Spiders feed on harmful insects. c.
   Rain soaks the spider's web. b.
   The spider stings the insect. a.
8. a, c
9. a spider to secure and build its web

The Red Army

1. necessary precondition
2. necessary precondition
3. no cause-effect
4. single cause
5. multiple causes
6. First, she lives on Christmas Island; second, she wants to protect her tires from crabs.
7. multiple causes
8. necessary precondition
9. c, b, a
10. a
11. d
12. The rains trigger the crabs' march to the sea.

Workhorses of the Desert

1. c
2. b
3. a. Its metabolic rate is low.
   b. It can eat low-grade, dry food.
   c. It can get along without water for two weeks or more.
4. a
5. Camels couldn't be used for transportation until they were tamed.
6. necessary precondition
7. Without its innately low metabolic rate, the camel would not be able to survive such intense heat.
8. necessary precondition
9. no cause-effect
10. There is no causal relationship between camels' dislike of work and their use as work-horses of the desert.
11. no cause-effect
12. All kinds of animals lose water, not just mammals.
13. single cause
14. The ability to eat low-grade food is due to the camel's low metabolic rate.

Follow-up Activities

1. Have students find cause-effect relationships on their own. Then have them describe the effect (like the fish got away) and see if the class can identify a cause.
2. Have students work in pairs and describe situations to illustrate no cause-effect relationships and multiple-cause relationships. Have pairs challenge their fellow students to identify the relationships illustrated by their stories.
3. Have students report on the behaviors of a specific animal and then try to relate one of the behaviors to the survival of the animal.
4. Help students create cause-effect relationships by using linking words—*so, therefore, because,* and *as a result.*
5. Set up two columns on the board. Label the first column *causes* and the second column *effects*. Write a few causes to get things started, such as "An oil spill," "Leaving toys

on the stairs," and "Finding money." Then challenge the class to list logical effects.

6. Challenge the class to list at least six pre-conditions that must be met before we can play basketball in the winter. (These might include reserving a gym, getting players, securing officials, choosing sides, securing a basketball, keeping score, and so on.)

V. Open Your Mind and Say "Ahh!": Understanding the Rules of Rational Thinking

Exercise I

1. false consolation
2. guilt by association
3. false consolation
4. appealing to friendship
5. guilt by association
6. appealing to friendship
7. appealing to false pride
8. appealing to friendship
9. guilt by association
10. appealing to friendship
11. appealing to false pride
12. false consolation
13. appealing to false pride
14. appealing to false pride
15. false consolation
16. guilt by association
17. false consolation
18. appealing to friendship
19. guilt by association
20. appealing to false pride

Exercise II

1. rationalization
2. gilding the truth
3. misuse of humor
4. gilding the truth
5. rationalization
6. strawman technique
7. strawman technique
8. misuse of humor
9. gilding the truth
10. rationalization
11. gilding the truth
12. misuse of humor
13. strawman technique
14. rationalization
15. strawman technique
16. misuse of humor
17. gilding the truth
18. rationalization
19. strawman technique
20. misuse of humor

Exercise III

1. stipulating a condition that isn't true
2. either-or
3. procrastination
4. slippery slope
5. stipulating a condition that isn't true
6. procrastination
7. slippery slope
8. either-or
9. slippery slope
10. stipulating a condition that isn't true
11. procrastination
12. either-or
13. slippery slope
14. stipulating a condition that isn't true
15. procrastination
16. either-or
17. stipulating a condition that isn't true
18. slippery slope
19. procrastination
20. either-or

Follow-up Activities

1. Ask students to write dialogues using fallacies. Then have classmates tell which fallacies were used.

2. Ask students to bring in examples of fallacies they see in print.

3. Clip examples of fallacies from newspapers or magazines. Challenge students to identify the fallacies.

VI. Too Good to Be True: Identifying Persuasive Techniques

Doll Treasures

b—Premier Grade; expert dollmaker; highest standards of craftsmanship

c—"only" $75.00; outstanding value

e—limited number; Certificate of Authenticity; signature of dollmaker; heirloom quality

g—seven U.S. presidents

l—limited number

1. *Top quality*—you could get made-in-Taiwan dolls at a fraction of the cost, but the dolls would be of inferior quality.

2. *Great savings*—the kind of people who would buy this product aren't usually concerned about money.

3. *Showing you care*—you could pass on the doll to your children to show them you really love them. (Other possible answers.)

4. Answers may vary. In general, it sounds like a top-quality product and a good deal, endorsed by famous people. Check for logic of answers.

A Multipurpose Wonder Blender

b—guaranteed

c—(first paragraph)

d—join your friends

f—(implied throughout the ad)

k—only 40 calories, creamy, healthful spread (there is a health appeal throughout ad)

1. Answers will vary. *Good for you* is pretty effective because it hits at something important to people—health and appearance.

2. Answers will vary. *Great savings* may be too great to be credible. *Bandwagon* may not be effective if the product is seen as cheap.

3. Various answers possible. Perhaps *Showing you care* could be used in terms of promoting the family's health through the use of this product.

4. Answers will vary. Look for logic behind answers and emphasize that responses should be based on the ad itself. Discuss other factors that could affect decisions.

United States Air Force Jacket

a—imagine yourself in one of these

b—premium, hand-stitched; methods called for by the USAF

g—(first paragraph)

j—six monthly installments

1. *Famous person*—this is what makes the jacket unique. *Snob appeal* is another possibility.

2. *Easy to own*—it makes the jacket sound cheap, as in a late-night TV offer, while the rest of the ad makes the jacket sound exclusive. Actually, the price is very high.

3. *Snob appeal*—showing how exclusive and "special" you would look in this jacket. Other possible answers.

4. Answers will vary. Check for logic behind answers.

The Best in the Business

b—(entire ad)

d—so many of your friends and neighbors in this community

h—agents are . . . just like you

i—plan a secure future for you and your family

k—do yourself a favor

1. *Good for you, showing you care, top quality*—these things are most important when it comes to life insurance.

2. *Bandwagon*—it shouldn't make a difference in the case of insurance.

3. None are clearly better choices, though students may suggest possibilities.

4. Answers will vary. One might say yes, but there are other considerations for buying insurance that are not clearly handled in the ad.

ASCOT Pens

b—best pen on the market; high quality

c—one free with a carton of 12 pens

e—both sides of your brain: your logical side, your creative side (*a* and *i* are also possibilities here)

l—limited-time offer

1. Answers will vary. The ad appeals to your sense of sophistication and quality. *Top quality, snob appeal,* and *glamorous you* are possibilities.

2. Answers will vary. The offer of the extra pen seems a little unnecessary for this type of product.

3. Answers will vary. Perhaps more emphasis on the quality of the pens, comparing it to the quality of others, would be effective.

4. Answers will vary. Look for logic behind responses and their relationship to the ad itself.

Pure Orange Juice Plus

b—30 percent RDA of calcium (merits of product described throughout ad)

g—coach of the U.S. Junior Olympics track-and-field team

i—healthy kids need healthy parents (the idea is pushed throughout ad)

k—strong and healthy; keep up our health and energy (implied throughout ad)

1. Answers may vary. *Good for you* is likely the most effective.

2. Answers may vary. None of the techniques is actually ineffective.

3. Answers will vary. Look for logic behind responses.

4. Answers will vary. Chances are that "Yes" is appropriate here. The product appeals to the "right" instincts in us.

Follow-up Activities

1. Have students find and explain persuasive techniques in print ads.

2. Challenge students to write an ad using persuasive techniques.

3. Have students write editorials about a current topic. Have volunteers share their editorials and challenge classmates to identify the persuasive techniques used.

4. Divide the class into pairs. Have each pair do a role-playing activity with one partner being a telephone solicitor and the other a thinking customer who challenges the telemarketer's persuasive techniques.

VII. The Writer Behind the Writing: Recognizing the Writer's Assumptions

Raising Fuel Standards

1. b

2. a. No; studies show that there is technology they are *not* using; justification not applicable.

   b. Yes; the author implies throughout the article that we need to save fuel; Yes; assumption is probably justified on the basis of outside information, news reports, and the like.

   c. Yes; they won't take advantage of technology to lower fuel use; Yes; justification may vary depending on students' background and point of view.

   d. No; this point is not mentioned in the article; justification is not applicable.

3. That the study is accurate and true

4. Answers will vary. Look for logic to support responses.

Misery Brings Success

1. c

2. a. Yes; author comes right out and says so in paragraph 2; No; other evidence and information show that some foods can be healthy and low-calorie and still taste good.

   b. No; author describes what you may order in a restaurant; justification not applicable.

   c. Yes; author actually says so; Yes; justification may vary; there may be other factors involved in weight loss.

   d. Yes; the author tells you to "think how noble you will feel"; Yes; the popular culture often equates slimness with well-being. Answers may vary.

3. They are not telling the truth. They are making promises in order to sell books, but the promises aren't reliable.

4. Answers will vary. Look for logic behind responses.

Exploring the Jungles of Africa

1. b
2. a. Yes; he faced many frightening hardships.
   b. Yes; he made intellectual contributions, including maps, analyses of diseases and possible treatments, and suggestions for commercial development.
   c. Yes; he made long-lasting contributions including maps for future travelers.
   d. Yes; he treated disease and did missionary work.
   e. Yes; he had a sympathetic view of other cultures and places that he would not have developed without curiosity.
   f. Yes; he survived hardships without outside resources.
   g. Yes; he stayed in Africa for many years.
   h. Yes; he was a missionary.

The Stories Behind Cave Paintings

1. b
2. a. Yes; they were not prepared to accept that the paintings were real without other evidence.
   b. Yes; they offered theories about the paintings.
   c. Yes; they could match and compare art from different places.
   d. Yes; they can only offer theories and do not claim certain knowledge.
   e. Yes; article refers to extinct animals, not fantasy creatures.
   f. No; no discussion of actual pace of work
   g. Yes; the article includes many positive references to art.

Keeping Kids Healthy

1. a
2. a. Answers may vary; the author implies this by the emphasis on physical education classes, but also notes that kids *are* fit; No; common sense says that other factors are also involved.
   b. Yes; author points out how little time is actually spent on physical activity; Yes; it makes sense to use time for actual physical activity.
   c. Yes; this is implied throughout; Yes; answers may vary, but we do seem to live according to habits picked up early in life.
   d. Yes; author notes that good fitness fights diseases, improves self-image, and so on; Yes; if these benefits are important to you, then the work is worth it.
3. They are probably unfit, and they might look into their child's physical education class. Other answers are possible.
4. Answers will vary. Look for logic behind responses.

Too Many Starlings?

1. c
2. a. No; author never says the population shouldn't be controlled, only how; justification not applicable.
   b. Yes; author seems to be saying that we ought to develop birth control for birds; Yes; it's harder to kill live birds when you can see them.
   c. No; author seems to imply that it is possible if we decide we want to; justification not applicable.
   d. Yes; author compares starlings with human immigrants; No; answers may vary, but the argument is not a strong one.
3. Their interest in profits keeps them from considering more humane alternatives.
4. Answers will vary. Check for logic behind responses.

Follow-up Activities

1. Ask each member of the class to clip one news item that represents a positive value and one that reflects a negative value. As a group, try to determine whether you agree with the reasoning behind one more than the other.
2. Form two debate teams and take different sides on controversial topics (teenage curfews, teenage employment, prayer before sporting events, and so on). Then have a panel identify unsupported assumptions that have been presented.
3. Examine several advertisements and look for exaggerations such as "the world's best" and

"indestructible." Then substitute more modest terms such as "good quality." Discuss the effect of these substitutions.

4. Many writers' faulty assumptions result from sweeping generalizations such as "Girls can't play sports," "People who don't have jobs are lazy," or "Everybody cheats." Challenge students to create a short list of these kinds of faulty assumptions.

5. Encourage students to write 10 generalizations that contain words such as "always," "all," "never," and "only." Then challenge them to rewrite the statements so that they are more reasonable and accurate.

6. Help students recognize how biased words can color generalizations. For example, if we use *cautious* instead of *cowardly*, *sentimental* instead of *mushy*, *courageous* instead of *reckless*, *young* instead of *immature*, *realistic* instead of *cynical*, and *compassionate* instead of *do-gooder*, we have a more acceptable presentation. Ask students to find examples of loaded language in print. Challenge the class to edit the examples so that the language is neutral.

Share Your Bright Ideas

We want to hear from you!

Your name_____Date_____

School name_____

School address_____

City _____State_____Zip_____Phone number (_____)_____

Grade level(s) taught_____Subject area(s) taught_____

Where did you purchase this publication?_____

In what month do you purchase a majority of your supplements?_____

What moneys were used to purchase this product?

_____School supplemental budget   _____Federal/state funding   _____Personal

Please "grade" this Walch publication in the following areas:

	A	B	C	D
Quality of service you received when purchasing	A	B	C	D
Ease of use	A	B	C	D
Quality of content	A	B	C	D
Page layout	A	B	C	D
Organization of material	A	B	C	D
Suitability for grade level	A	B	C	D
Instructional value	A	B	C	D

COMMENTS:_____

_____

What specific supplemental materials would help you meet your current—or future—instructional needs?

_____

Have you used other Walch publications? If so, which ones?_____

May we use your comments in upcoming communications?   _____Yes   _____No

Please **FAX** this completed form to **888-991-5755**, or mail it to

Customer Service, Walch Publishing, P. O. Box 658, Portland, ME 04104-0658

We will send you a **FREE GIFT** in appreciation of your feedback. **THANK YOU!**